CDR Unlimited Publishing
P.O. Box 16141, Memphis TN 38186

Cover and Interior Design: Ambicionz
www.ambicionz.com

Mountain Movers/C. Denise Richardson — 1st ed.
ISBN 978-1537373973

Mountain Movers

MOVING MOUNTAINS AND TAKING NAMES

C. Denise Richardson

CDR UNLIMITED PUBLISHING
P.O. Box 16141
Memphis, TN 38186

Contents

DEDICATION

I dedicate this book to my one authentic love, Cedric and my four daughters Tee, Bri, Rae, LC and of course my former self, "Carolyn". Thank you beautiful people for allowing me to share parts of your story and for your continued love and support.

Romans 8:28 is our family's strength.

ACKNOWLEDGEMENTS

Life Changers Church Family: For all the spiritual challenges, sleepless nights, joyful days, and push to greatness! You all have blessed me tremendously. I never knew how much a God inspired vision could stretch me! Thanks for staying the course!

Paula Geeter: For your friendship, love, encouragement and constructive criticism! You're an amazing woman! I remember you once said, "You're a strong woman. You inspire me girl. Whew". Thanks for the push, both the verbal and non-verbal.

Sandra Stokes: You've been with me for the long haul! You've inspired me in ways that no one else has! I remember you saying, "Rich, people miss the quality of friendship with you because they just can't get past your outer shell...your looks". I'm thankful that you got it! Three decades of friendship. Love you doll.

Angela McDowell: AW, I thank God for our divine connection. You've inspired, loved, chastised and admired me. You're not a huge talker...opposites attract, but you've spoken volumes with your actions of love, trust, and faith in God toward me. It's indeed a blessing to know that you're a lifetime confidant!

Doreen Harper: Doe, our meeting was not luck, chance or fate. It was all part of God's divine plan and trajectory to both greatness and destiny! Doreen Harper, thank you for believing God concerning me and my RICH purpose!!! I remember you saying to me, "Denise, listen...woosah. You're amazing and you're gonna be fine."

Latita Harrison: Lord, thank you for always questioning everything and anything. You continue to stretch me and it's a blessing to know that I inspire you to live your purpose in the "now" season. Kingdom blessings in all you do according to His plans for your life.

FOREWORD
BY: PAULA GEETER

Sometimes in our lives as little girls, our innocence is shattered seemingly beyond repair by Satan through [his] tactics of physical, emotional, psychological, or sexual abuse. In spite of the turmoil we experience from our past, many little girls grow into women living life in and on purpose. I'm almost certain that although it's undeniably painful to confront the mountains of our pasts, it's quite liberating to do so! Question, what mountain paralyzes you with a fear so great that you sense the heaviness of it whenever you think about it?

The ability to push past the fear to unlock the buried treasures of greatness reveals a greater truth about the greatness within [you] through Christ Jesus! I call this the "Passion Principle"! The passion to excel! The passion to exceed (one's own limitations and the limitations of others)! The passion to grow! The passion to transform (from the caterpillar to the beautiful butterfly)! The passion to set your goals high enough that you must audaciously trust God Himself has to elevate you there! Your passion proves greater than the pain you previously experienced. Now that's amazing! You're amazing! The dream is amazing!

However, if those dreams are shattered, we tend to break commitments because of the mental and spiritual rejection the enemy has placed in our minds. Moreover, attempting to develop healthy, loving relationships for Jesus Christ, family, friends, co-workers or even our mates appear unattainable due to our fragmented healing. Additionally, our lack of spiritual, mental, and physical development impedes our assiduous efforts to accomplish those important things in life because of our past.

Contrariwise, some women abandon purpose due, in part, to the pain they've endured. The pain of their pasts plagues them so much so that, the mountain "appears" insurmountable and that is much more frightening! These women lose sight of both God and their individual purposes! Purposes rich in promise and pain! Hey, the struggle is most definitely "Rich"! I Peter 3:14 assures us that suffering for Christ has its benefits! What better reward than to live victoriously despite the numerous mountains encountered!

As we examine our pasts, there is a cause and effect factor to our deteriorating spirits and non-purposeful living which have led many of us to neglect praying to God about who we are in Christ, but rather to engage in undesirable behaviors, appearances and conversations. The cause is in our consciousness (mind) which is unseen because it is where Satan can place negative thoughts about us. The effect are the circumstances in our lives in which we can see and visibly express - our mistakes, addictive behaviors, inappropriate attire, unprotected sexual behaviors/habits and other compromising behaviors that can lead one to get what she wants regardless of who she hurts. However, there is a cure through the love and transformation power of Jesus Christ in our lives. Ephesians 1:11 (MSG) says," It's in Christ that we find out who we are and what we are living for. Long before we first heard of

Christ...He had His eye on us, had designs on us for glorious living, part of the overall purpose He is working out in everything and everyone".

Dr. C. Denise Richardson is a beautiful woman who is purpose-driven by climbing over the many mountains in her life with Jesus Christ. She is a woman of God who shares her testimony of how her transformational experiences and intimate relationship with Jesus Christ gave her purpose, peace, love, deliverance, direction, strength, and prosperity to live a life of total commitment to God. Even though her life has not been perfect, she believes in pressing pass her situation through serving Jesus Christ with all her heart and mind through her daily prayers. Her story will show you how much God loves you through any circumstances and the plans He has for your life, but it requires commitment and dedication to Jesus Christ.

THE RICHEST BACKSTORY

As a CSA survivor, I've experienced each mountain discussed in this book. My initial encounter with sexual abuse occurred when I was approximately four years old. I've attempted to recall if it was my mother's sibling, who requested that I lick his penis "like a lollipop" or, my maternal aunt's [then] boyfriend. Either way, my innocence was slowly dissipating and no one seemed to care or notice.

Ladies, please know that you are not alone! You are not the only one who has endured sexual abuse, through no fault of your own. No, you did not "ask for it"! I didn't ask to be molested by a relative's lover. Nor did I request that he spend countless hours alone with me further damaging my emotional, psychological, and spiritual being! I was facing numerous mountains at such a young age. I was ill equipped to mount or move such a formidable mountain.

Unbeknownst to me, sexual abuse was a mountain familiar to my family. A familiar mountain that no one discussed or confronted. These are the types of mountains no one boldly faces, prophetically speaks to, or fearlessly climbs! See, that's the thing! I've been so psychologically damaged that I just believe God to do the amazing in my life!

I erroneously believed that although some mountains were familiar territory, I'd be able to confront and conquer them effortlessly. My goodness, was I wrong! The mountains were familiar but, definitely not the same! The familiar mountains were only familiar because some of the people, circumstances, or encounters were the same. We must remember that although the mountains appear to be the same, God's word also remains unchanging! What a blessing! God is definitely consistent in maintaining both His word and His promises [to you]!

If your backstory resembles mine, you understand the urgency in which we must confront our mountains. Generational sexual abuse is far too common, especially in the homes of Christians. Maybe you've struggled with forgiveness or even the perplexity of each mountain you've faced. Don't allow the challenging of your faith to cause you to buckle. Remember, you were built for this! You were born to win! Christ overcame [even] death!

Mountains represent the challenges in our lives. The challenges range from childhood experiences to present day circumstances. If allowed, mountains overshadow purpose and passion. [Our] determination must eclipse any signs of overwhelming fear. I say overwhelming fear because as humans some fear is to be expected. The fear should never be greater than our faith in Him. Now understand this, fear and faith cannot exist simultaneously. However, the experience of fear is alright, in and of itself. One must exercise caution not to allow that emotion full control! This could prove problematic and ultimately detrimental to moving the mountain. Are you ready to move your mountain(s)? Let's do it!

"What are you, O great mountain? Before Zerubbabel you will become a plain; and he will bring forth the top stone with shouts of "Grace, grace to it!" - Zechariah 4:7

The mountains we encounter often appear insurmountable. However, it is in God's strength through Christ Jesus that we are able to speak to the mountains impeding our lives. We are equipped to speak to them to move! We have the authority to speak to the mountains of generational curses and fear that subtly inundate our lives. Mountains are meant to be climbed or (re)moved.

Songs have been masterfully penned and powerfully sung about God giving the believer "strength" to climb mountains, and they are most certain to arise during the course of one's life. I'm one to enjoy the triumphs of those who strategically plan, painstakingly prepare, and triumphantly climb natural (physical) mountains.

There are those who enjoy the thrill of climbing to the peaks of Mt. Everest, Kilimanjaro, Makalu, or K2. Women of all walks of life meet the challenge of climbing these mountains with great excitement. Contrariwise, believers, when faced with larger than life mountains, tend to shy away from their God given purpose. Despair, despondency, and even depression often overwhelm the believer. Purpose is neither birthed nor nurtured when the believer elects to operate in fear (of the mountain). In order for purpose to manifest, mountains must be moved. Sometimes the prayers of others, through God's grace, aids in the purpose shaking process. There remain others who view mountain climbing as a tedious, irrelevant factor that need not be welcomed or experienced. Nonetheless, I suppose that mountain climbing (whether literal or spiritual) can be an exhilarating trajectory during one's journey to destiny!

As a young girl growing up in rural Arkansas, I was exposed to so much at an early age. My mother completed high school & entered college. She was a determined young lady. She climbed her mountains, mountains of low self-esteem, mountains of rejection, mountains of being motherless at the young age of thirteen, mountains of being an unwed, pregnant teen, mountains of despair & uncertainty. My mother didn't realize it then, but she was moving mountains, shaking and awakening purpose in those around her!

That's the thing! As women of the word, we should always commit to shaking purpose in others whether we do so intentionally or unintentionally! We must awaken & shake purpose. When we encounter women in our daily experiences, purpose must be allowed to thrive. When we remain bound in the things that initially imprisoned us, we are ill-equipped, broken, spiritually distorted, fragments of who we should be. Many of my mother's mountains were inherently passed on to me, her unsuspecting, beautiful daughter. Now, her mountains have become mine, and I've been climbing them ever since.

Unbeknownst to many believers, some mountains are present in our lives in the womb. The mountains are not meant to discourage or limit us, but rather to strengthen our faith...in Him. The mountains affect our perspective. The manner in which we perceive the mountain contributes to our success or apparent failure in climbing or moving the mountain altogether.

The significance of any mountain becomes relative to the individual climbing it. If the individual possesses a distorted view of God or life, then he or she most assuredly views the mountain negatively. A predisposition to dysfunctional environments and negative conversations often contribute to our inability to speak to mountains while simultaneously trusting God [by faith] to move it!

I've long believed (through divine revelation and scripture) that our battles with mountains begin while we are innocent, accepting, carefree youth! However, at some point in our lives; we begin to transform. Our minds are no longer as carefree as they once were. Our innocence is compromised by some experience during the formative years of our youth. Experiences of mental, verbal, physical, sexual abuse or any combination of the four shape our views, often times with contaminated perceptions.

The mountains represent the various challenges we encounter. To the believer, mountains mustn't represent intimidation through fear but rather accomplishment through faith. How a believer perceives the mountain is critical. It's literally the difference between victory and defeat! I am fully persuaded that He Who has begun a good work in [each] of us, will perform it until the day of Jesus Christ. The greatness within us, once unlocked, challenges our faith to move toward action! Guess what? Mountain moving requires action! We must "do" something along with speaking.

The late Tammy Terrell and Marvin Gaye sang a love ballad about moving mountains! Love motivated by love! The song inspires listeners to push passed the obstacles, tumultuous situations, or life hacks in order to reach the one they love! What a beautiful sentiment...and song! Then, Miley Cyrus challenges [her] listeners to view the mountain as an adventure! What a beautiful song to inspire listeners to see the potential of the mountain climb. The potential to conquer the mountain offers hope within the challenge itself! Wow! Miley's lyrics paint a picture of fortitude and [inner] determination! Are you determined?

WHY MOUNTAINS

With at least 500 Biblical mentions, mountains are definitely relevant! Their literal and symbolic meanings demonstrate their significance in the lives of those who love God. In

Old Testament scripture, Jehovah reveals Himself numerous times atop various mountains. Wow! Can you imagine "The Creator" [of the universe] atop a mountain revealing His will to His chosen men?! This is so amazing [to me]. God!

Mountains are mentioned in both the New and Old Testaments. Mountains represent many life changing experiences. Mountains reveal the disruption within the earth. Similarly, mountains in our lives reveal on the outside a buildup or unsettlement within us. Mountains represent challenges. Challenges represent difficulties, possible defeat and fear of the unknown. The average individual resists difficulty when possible! Question, are you "average" or are you the exception to the rule?

With difficulty comes the challenge to be stretched in areas of comfortability and complacency. After all, mountains are massive structures that require strength, fortitude, and accountability [primarily to one's self]. When we face the mountains of our lives, we are agreeing to take charge, to become responsible, to become accountable for the results and overall outcomes. Furthermore, we can no longer remain isolated, indifferent or fearful. The mountains require the "climber" to take action. This may initially prove difficult. However, the ability to face the mountain and; consequently, conquer or move it becomes the motivation to actually conquer it!

Throughout the New Testament Jesus is seen praying in the mountains. Some of His most difficult challenges occurred while in the mountains. It was in the mountains that He was tempted of Satan to jump from the cliff [of the mountain]. Matthew and Luke record and recount Jesus' teaching of the "Beatitudes", typically known as the "Sermon on the Mount". Jesus' "moral teaching" from the mountain reveals yet again the significance of every mountain we encounter! The mountain, or its enormity, did not intimidate Jesus. Similarly, we must acknowledge and possibly evaluate the mountain while forging ahead to complete the task before us! The mountain, nor its size prevented Jesus from delivering God's message to His people. Yes, the climb may have been challenging and extremely exhausting. But, purpose was more important! Purpose fuels passion! Are you ready to face your mountains...with a revised perspective? I am! I will! I do! I shake and awaken the passionate purpose within!

The experience of moving mountains is often tagged with a price. And that price, in many instances, is quite exorbitant! The price is way too hefty for most! However, those who are obsessively passionate about purpose invariably and unapologetically move [their] mountains! It's almost second nature to the natural born mountain mover to instinctively and consistently anticipate moving the next mountain before it arises! Mountain Movers recognize the distinction between conquering mountains and moving mountains! Oh, make no mistakes; seasoned mountain movers no longer fear facing their mountains! They fearlessly welcome the opportunity to overcome that someone else may be inspired to conquer (or move) their mountain(s)!

The Bible awakens all believers to the certainty of mountains! As uneasy as it may be to acknowledge, troubles, in the form of mountains, arise! Troubles are certain yet conquerable...through Him who rose from the dead! Even a staunch faith walker may find it difficult to joyfully welcome troubles. However, scripture states the following irrefutable truth, "Consider it all joy, my brethren, when you encounter various trials, knowing that the testing of your faith produces endurance. And let endurance have its perfect result, so that you may be perfect and complete, lacking in nothing". Are you prepared (spiritually, mentally, and physically equipped) to move mountains?

CHAPTER 1

EMOTIONAL MOUNTAINS

"The best and most beautiful things in the world cannot be seen or even touched. They must be felt with the heart" - Helen Keller

The pain of emotional mountains hijack our sense of purpose due, in part, to our close heart/mind connections. What we think and believe springs from our heart, whether guarded or unguarded. - C. Denise

"Emotional roller coaster...", We've all heard the song, know of someone who's heard the song or have heard the phrase to describe a time period in someone's life; but emotional roller coasters are much more serious than the truism in which it is. Emotional roller coasters aren't like the fun roller coasters you look forward to riding at your local amusement park. Unlike these roller coasters, you don't have the luxury of hopping off when the ride is over with little to no side effects. In fact, once off an emotional roller coaster the side effects appear to be only the beginning of a life long struggle with defeat. Emotions range not only in type but also degree in which they thwart your productivity in life. From sadness and loneliness to anger and resentment, emotional mountains can seem like the worst thing to ever present itself in your life. But there is hope. There is a proverbial "silver lining" at the end of the day because we possess hope for a better tomorrow. This hope lies in Christ and in Him alone. Acknowledging and eventually confronting the emotional mountains in your life can mean the difference between living a life of peace or living a life of pain.

REJECTION/ABANDONMENT

No one revels in rejection unless he or she lives a life of chaos or dysfunction. The mere thought sends chills down the spines of men and women alike. The thought of rejection by someone you care for deeply may cause inward emotions to manifest outwardly in a variety of ways, such as sweaty palms and a racing heartbeat. But the truth of the matter is, that this romanticized version of rejection is simply not as bad as it gets. Fear of rejection begins long before elementary school crushes and pre-adult proposals. The sense of belonging and being wanted starts from the very moment of conception and is why recognizing this particular mountain and moving it, is so vital to anyone who seeks to live a life of peace and joy.

When a mother conceives a child, her attitude toward the pregnancy largely contributes to how the child will not only respond to the mother, but also to life in general. If a mother harbors unresolved issues be it positive or negative, towards the father, it influences the child dramatically (spiritually and naturally). Physicians promote healthy emotional interaction, development and wellbeing because it is conducive to the comprehensive social and emotional wellbeing of the infant during pregnancy. And more importantly, why do you think God emphasizes marriage before procreating? There's a direct correlation and deeper meaning for it all! If it didn't matter it wouldn't be so important. God knew the risk men and women would take in doing things opposite the way He'd planned.

When a mother carries a child for 9-10 months while going through emotional woes with the father or with herself, she does not allocate the time to cherish and embrace the miracle happening within her. If her feelings toward the father include anger and frustration she then places herself in the possible predicament to express these feelings toward her child prior to birth (spiritually speaking). As the child grows and gets older, that innate desire to bond with the mother and love on her turns into unrequited love and, eventually results in feelings of outright rejection.

I can remember as a child never experiencing the personal love and care I desired from my mother. I attempted to do any and every thing to please her, to somehow make her love me in ways I could not define, but nothing ever seemed to be good enough. Some of my methods, although unorthodox, were desperate attempts to gain both her attention and approval.

Even well into my adult years, I would sacrifice time with my husband and children to cater to the needs of my mother in order to try to somehow have the love I so often expressed to her reciprocated to me. It wasn't until I realized that the mountain of rejection and abandonment I'd felt from my mother had caused this molehill to become a "Mount Everest" in my life. It was painful to accept [the reality] that my mother had not only allowed her unaddressed feelings from her own childhood to cripple her ability to bond and connect with me, but she'd abandoned and rejected me in her neglecting to do so. I [had] sacrificed years of my life trying to "fix" something within her that only Christ could repair. Once I realized that this mountain had blinded me and allowed me to become controlled by my emotions I knew there was only one way to move it. I had to look it head on and tell [Satan] and rejection that they no longer had power in my life.

The liberty I experienced by releasing the pressure from this emotional mountain once I'd let it go was indescribable. I was able to refocus on my marriage, my parenting, and my dreams. I'm almost certain that I'm not alone. I make this bold statement because so many adult women struggle with "who" they are and, I believe this is a direct correlation to their "mother/daughter" relationship growing up. When mothers feel the pressure to choose between career and mothering, children are often the ones who suffer...or "lose". A child or, more importantly, daughter loses when she does not form a positive, thriving, productive relationship with her "same sex" parent.

Many times when we have been rejected by a parent we respond by trying to win their love and affection by our acts of devotion to them. God does not encourage this practice! God freely and unconditionally loves every individual He created. It is His good pleasure to do so. Moreover, Jeremiah 31:3 reads, *"The LORD hath appeared of old unto me, saying, Yea, I have loved thee with an everlasting love: therefore with lovingkindness have I drawn thee".* This scripture gives me life! I'm hopeful.

I found myself aiding and abetting the very sins I spoke out against, all in an effort to experience the love I so desired from my mother. Once I allowed God to chisel away at the mountain and break it down to the point in which I could now mount it, I vowed to never again allow the feeling of rejection or abandonment to have rule and authority in my life ever again!

For instance, if I didn't secure the job or position I desired, if I wasn't accepted by the group of people I assumed to be potential acquaintances, feelings of rejection couldn't trouble me, because that mountain in my life had been moved. Sooner or later we must face the fact that we've been affected by the emotional mountain of rejection and it's up to each individual to choose to trust God and command that mountain to move. I realized that I could have allowed these feelings to significantly influence the way I interacted with my husband and children. Anything could potentially trigger my responses to be those of negativity and anger toward the family I loved so dearly. I did not desire to be a cold, distant, unhappy woman. So, I began to ask God to work on me. The angry, self-loathing, unhappy woman who, by many accounts, was beautiful (on the outside) required a spiritual makeover!

In one aspect I could have easily interacted with conspicuous noninvolvement and disinterest while on the other hand I could have been overly involved and controlling [of them] causing them to distance themselves from me. I'd resolved in my mind to be the mother that God created me to be. Needless to say, errors were made and missteps occurred. Standing firm in my convictions without compromise has given me much joy and the peace is sweet. The joy and peace that I've enjoyed didn't come without a price though.

I can remember being overwhelmed with thoughts of pleasing her while simultaneously disliking "who" she was to others and "who" she couldn't be [for me...my mother]. By God's grace, I was able to recognize the control I'd given this mountain and by doing so I was able to live the life God pre-destined me to live with those who meant the most to me. It's a choice. It's an intentional decision to identify [the rejection mountain], acknowledge [the pain], and decide [to conquer the mountain] of emotional dysfunction. We must choose to move this mountain of rejection or it will, in fact, move you from one place to the next.

LOW-SELF WORTH

Someone once said "your value is decreased based on someone's inability to see your worth". However, the reality of this crass statement should NEVER be the case for believ-ers. When someone doesn't view you for who you really are and all the potential you have, it eventually results in feelings of rejection and unworthiness...if you buy into it. Low self-worth or low self-esteem is a mountain that troubles men, women, boys and girls alike. A young lady recently shared with me the following, "she never really believed that you would be the great woman that you are or who God has called you to be...she gave up on God's plan for you". This was troubling on many levels because I was blindsided. This statement was more profound because the "she" was my biological mother. This was the "wake up" of a lifetime. I'd known others who eagerly wrote me off, but not my [own] mother!

Many times this mountain stems from the mountain of re-jection or abandonment. When we feel we are not good enough for someone, we begin to define our worth based on other people's ability to accept us as we are. When you've suf-fered from years of rejection, the reality of the rejection be-comes more difficult to endure. It's a very disheartening reality; however, many people dedicate years altering who they are both internally and externally, only to find that they are still unhappy.

I can recall entering relationships with men who didn't value the true beauty within me. As I meditate on this memory, I realize that I didn't value the beauty within myself. Because I didn't value myself, due to a myriad of factors, I entered an abusive, self-defeating relationship with a dysfunctional guy who physically and emotionally abused me. This experience (another mountain that I'd created) made me feel even less confident in myself than before. After finally ending this relationship, I entered into another one with a man who was unable to appreciate me and was also emotionally and psychologically abusive. You see, when you don't see God's value in yourself there's no way you can expect others to see that value. But that's where we fail all too often. We desperately crave man's approval and validation as opposed to our Creator's.

God validated you when He knit you in your mother's womb. He expressed His love for you and your worth in this world when He sent Jesus to die on the cross at Calvary for your sins. Satan tells you to doubt your self-worth, that you are unworthy of man's love therefore you are unworthy of Gods. But God tells us that He in fact loved you so much He sent His one and only Son to die just for you! Low self-worth and Satan tell you that you were a mistake. God tells you that you were birthed with purpose and that He knows the exact plans He has for your life.

Satan and low self-worth subtly whisper in your spirit that you are not good enough, not smart enough, not beautiful enough. God tells you that you were fearfully and wonderfully made in His own image. When you realize where your worth and treasure lie, no man on earth, devil in hell, nor mountain before you can even attempt to make you believe a lie. God desires to see His creations full of the confidence and authority He placed in them. Too often, unresolved issues of rejection and abandonment result in facing mountains of low self-worth. But believe as I personally had to believe, within your heart, that God has already given you His stamp of approval and you are His delight.

Accepting this truth in your mind and heart releases you from the feelings of unworthiness and Satan's lies affording you the power to move the mountain of low self-worth and poor decision making. The mountain of low self-worth tells you things are impossible because you don't deserve it. God says that even the things you **DON'T** deserve are made possible through Him. Believe this truth and move this mountain that has imposed control in your life far longer than it should have!

Depression/Suicide

When feelings of rejection and low self-worth continue, unaddressed, and the mountains continue to have precedence in your life, it can and most times will result in you facing the mountain of depression and suicide. Although I have not personally experienced this mountain I know far too many individuals who have and currently do face it. I often times find myself very randomly thanking God that through all the chaos and mountains, I have indeed had to face that He has protected me from this mountain. God wants us to know that we are more than conquerors through Christ Jesus and because of this we can overcome anything and everything through faith in Jesus. We don't have to succumb to pressures of death because Christ has already come to earth, lived, and died for us.

Depression doesn't have to defeat you. Suicide doesn't have to be the only option for you. This mountain seeks to instill so much regret, resentment and anger within you that you have no choice but to give in to its every whim. The Bible tells us that Satan comes to steal, kill, and destroy. This is true in both a figurative and literal sense. If he can steal the peace you have in your life, kill the hope you once found in Christ, and destroy the desire you had to pursue your purpose, it's that much easier to steal, kill, and destroy, your very being. Jesus came and showed us that through God's word we have the ability to defend ourselves and combat the enemy's tactics and schemes. Putting on the full armor of God and studying His word that we may know how to fight against the temptation of depression are the fundamental principles and practices to moving this mountain.

Moving this resistant mountain definitely won't be easy. Depression places one in a state of mind where there is a lack of hope and an oasis of fear and doubt. The way you combat this is not by getting medications to numb the situation, but by receiving the truth of God to overcome those thoughts. Satan knows that if he can gain access to attack the mind and cause feelings as though nothing in life is worth fighting for, he can cause us to turn away from God.

Depression begins in our minds. It may be depression onset by poor decisions you made or it may be onset by the actions of someone else, whatever the case, depression does not have to defeat you. When we allow depression to overtake and consume us. Prescription pills, retail therapy, and other vices deemed to remedy the problem don't thwart the thoughts and fears from resurfacing or lingering on we're paralyzed by yet another mountain. Depression inevitably torments those battling this debilitating disease. Joyce Meyer's bestselling book "Battlefield of the Mind", challenges readers to retrain the brain in an effort to live a life conducive to wholeness and wellness? Are you committed to living a "**RICH**ly balanced" life?

Satan is effective in going beyond the ease a pill may bring. He recognizes it's not until you seek the spiritual root of the cause that you will receive the breakthrough you so desire. Too often individuals refuse to seek the necessary professional assistance needed to overcome specific mountains.

John 10:10 in the new King James Version reads *"The thief cometh not but to steal and to kill and to destroy. I am come that they might have life, and that they might have it more abundantly."* Depression and suicide are Satan's prescriptions for dealing with life's hard times, peace and joy are God's. It may seem impossible to have joy and have peace in the midst of hard times, but when God is your source for life and purpose nothing is impossible. Overcome depression with dependency on God.

Defeat suicidal thoughts with the truth of salvation. The mountains of depression and suicide will be moved when erroneous thinking transforms to spiritually cognitive thinking. When praying your prayer of mountain moving concerning depression and suicide remember and reference Romans 8:6 *"For to set the mind on the flesh is death, but to set the mind on the Spirit is life and peace."* Allow these words to minister to you even now as you read these words: "I am an overcomer. I am dead to the sin and temptation of depression and suicidal thoughts and I am free from the mountain of depression and suicide. Satan you nor it, have control over me or my life! In Jesus' Name, Amen." Question, are you prepared to actively engage in protecting your mind and thoughts from the lies Satan presents?

CHAPTER 2

FINANCIAL MOUNTAINS
CONTRIBUTED BY: GABRIELLE CRUMP

"You've got to tell your money what to do or it will leave."
- Dave Ramsey

It's no surprise that finances are usually number one on the list of challenges that make or break relationships of all types. Husbands and wives divorce because one or the other, or sometimes even both, mismanaged finances. Business partners who were longtime friends end up enemies for the rest of their lives because of finances. Children and parents become estranged because a loan was given but never repaid. There's no wonder why one of the most quoted scriptures of the bible is 1Tim. 6:10. Often times misquoted the scripture reads: ***"For the LOVE of money is a root to all kinds of evil..."*** Many people become perplexed as to why a seemingly sweet,

caring, and loving individual could resort to murdering someone over an insurance policy or unpaid bill. Scripture explains
it as clear as day. When a person loves money, it gives life to
all sorts of evils. But not all financial strains are as extreme.
Sometimes it may be losing someone or even worse (in my
opinion) their trust because the mountain of finances was
never conquered. What causes the mountain of finances to go
from being the hill we slid down on as a child to the Mt. Everest so many die trying to climb?

THE "MY MONEY" MOUNTAIN

Financial mountains come in the form of many different
challenges for many different people. The "My Money" men-
tality is one that peaks at some point in many relationships.
They tower over us as a means of reminding us just how little
control we have in our very own lives. Take for example the
couple in their first year of marriage. The young duo are eager
to embark on a life long journey of fun, love and "happily ever
after." Things are seemingly going to plan until one day the
"My Money" insult shoots out of the mouth of the hardwork-
ing breadwinner.

The ideal "fairytale" storyline quickly shifts into a nightmare no one was prepared for. Angry words go back and forth
about hours worked and time spent building the empire of a
business that brings home the funds used to splurge on life's
finer things. For this couple, the mountain of finances is much
bigger than they may realize. When one person, in a two-per-
son relationship, be it marital, friendship, or business, feels
more entitled to money; it causes a rift in that relationship. A
homemaker may feel inferior. The business partner may feel
as if they have less stock in the business. And the friend may

feel as if their friendship now hangs in the balance. Overcoming the "my money" mountain may seem difficult to move but with the practice of three God-given habits, the miles high mountain becomes the "mountain conquered!"

My first year of marriage was centered on many arguments about money. Many times I found myself sad in spirit because I never knew just how big a deal money was to my husband. Many times men find a sense of self-worth in how much money they have. Women find security in knowing that her spouse is able to provide the basic necessities needed to sustain the family.

The issue for me came when my husband felt as if he, as the primary breadwinner, did not have to share the details of our financial situation. When arguments would occur he would always resort to saying that he was not "used to having to share those details." For so long "he" had been in full control of the money matters of his life. That's a note to consider from my own testimony when entering into marriage, when you submit to God and the way He structures things "me and I", truly become "us and we".

It wasn't until closer to our second year of marriage that my husband saw the need to incorporate me in our financial status. As his wife and partner I had to stress the fact that it was I he asked to marry him and with that came the responsibility to keep me in the know. It took many conversations and much prayer to help us understand that money did not have to be a mountain in our marriage and that the mountain that had formed was not too big for us to conquer.

The first objective that needs to be overcome is admitting there is an issue. Had my husband never confessed his need to be in control of the finances in our marriage and how difficult it was for him to let me in, we never would have been able to tackle the mountain of finances the way we did. A shopaholic, drinker, smoker, and gambler all have one thing in common: the affect the money spent to support these bad habits have on them and their families.

If you can't admit and acknowledge to God, yourself, and those you care about just how big the mountain is you'll never be able to climb it. No one ever wakes up one morning and decides "Hey, I will climb Mt. Everest today." without first acknowledging that it is a mountain that is BIG and requires a plan of action in order to climb. In the same manner if we don't admit how out of control money (in whatever capacity) has become in our lives.

Most times we create the financial mountains in our lives by acting without praying and waiting for God to respond. We move before He gives confirmation. We buy the home, the car, or invest in a business because at the moment it looks and sounds good. We neglect to give into God's kingdom, and we often times out right disobey Gods instructional wisdom. When we do things without consulting God first, especially when it comes to money, we begin forming those financial mountains that torture us many years of our lives.

The second objective to overcome is the communication barrier. Often times in relationships a misunderstanding in communication occurs. A new husband can communicate with his new wife how he plans to use finances in the marriage. Keeping his wife in the know regarding bank account balances, bills, debt, etc. can mean the difference in a happy healthy marriage and one built on a lack of trust. This also makes the wife truly feel like part of the team. Even if she is a working wife, or if the husband stays home and the wife works, communication is crucial and critical to the financial longevity in any marriage. Business partners can communicate the importance of finances in the business. Creating a 5-

year plan is one way to ensure that the money put into the business and acquired by the business benefits both parties and one partner is not left feeling alone. If one business partner has to put funds on the table for startup costs communicate any and all expectations of repayment or a form of reciprocity. Friends can write contracts and have an understanding in both verbal and written form that there is an expectation of repayment. Sometimes tough conversations have to be had, but in order to reach that peak, you have to face the wind head on.

The third and final objective is becoming more obedient. One night, unable to sleep, I went to God and simply asked Him how my family could overcome the financial mountain we'd created. He spoke three steps we needed to put into practice in order to mount the mountain of finances in our lives. The problem often times always stems from a lack of obedience, a lack of trust, and a great deal of fear, that paralyze us into thinking if we don't do with our money as we please then our lives are lived in vain. That's simply not the case, or should not be the case for the believer. Transforming attitudes about (God's) money is what differentiates good stewards from poor stewards. God spoke as clear as I had heard Him in quite some time about the steps that not only should be taken, but had to be taken, in order to conquer our financial mountain. I began following the steps with my husband and immediately began to see results and encourage you to adapt these life changing steps into your own life.

The first step is: SOWING. When it comes to finances for any follower of Christ our first priority should never be "me" but "them". How am I blessing someone else who has needs far greater than mine? Sowing is not just giving to your local church. God speaks to those who are willing to listen. And God will speak to those who believe in Him, in the area of sowing.

When you sow, or pour financially into someone who God speaks to your heart, you not only take a step toward obedience, but also showing God that you trust Him to provide for you. Consider the poor widow found in Mark 12:44. She stood back and watched as many rich men poured out their wealth from their abundance, but instead of feeling intimidated or worrying about how **SHE** would make ends meet, she trusted God and "gave everything---all she had to live on." We can't fully be who God has called us to be in the area of finance if we aren't willing to give of our last. God sees our hearts when decide to trust Him completely with the money He blesses us with. The first way to do that is to begin sowing wherever He may lead you. It could be to sow into your local ministry, maybe sowing more than you have been. It could be sowing into the single mom, recently divorced woman, the young man seeking a job, or the poor widow who has very little. When you obey God and sow, He honors it.

The second step is: SAVE. "A lot easier said than done!" my husband would so frequently argue. Saving in a one income home with a wife, two children, and bills by the boat load, seems impossible to do to those who have little faith. Saving just like sowing requires obedience, discipline, and faith! And as believers who desire to move, mount, or climb the financial mountains in our lives, we must realize the importance of saving. Savings not only set up future security for you and immediate family, but by practicing the principle of saving God's way you leave an inheritance for your future generations. Proverbs 13:22 is a great exert on why saving is and should be a priority in those trying to move the mountain of finance. When we think about life in terms of our future the frivolous spending becomes menial. Lots of times we fall into the pattern of "buying with our eyes" and big business knows this. We go to the grocery store with the intent to purchase one thing and leave with twenty more items than we needed. Christmas time is used as a way to spend more money than we have because we attempt to impress and over compensate instead of focusing on its true meaning. We put money aside only to spend it on things we don't need later. We eat out instead of cooking in and saving a few dollars that way. Then when someone is in need or we ourselves face emergencies, we don't have our own secure backup plan. God does not intend for us to borrow but to lend (Prov. 22:7) and to be great stewards over the things in which He's entrusted to us. Saving is a best practice because it prepares us for our future as well as our children and their children. People don't save because they can't; they don't because they refuse to see it as a priority. Set a weekly or monthly amount to save and then do it! Five dollars a week can turn into $260 in one year. A higher dollar amount equals a higher year end amount. Start saving and see your mountain move.

The final step is: SPEND. When you practice the first two in that order the last step is spending. But before you get too excited "spending" may not be what you think. The spending step is broken up into three subcategories: immediate bills, debt, and personal allowance. Most of our mountains form because we don't prioritize our finances. We give ourselves a personal allowance first, followed by our bills being paid, and if we have money to spare we give that to prior debts. Prioritizing your "spend" account will be the difference between debt freedom and being in debt over your head. If you don't properly manage your spending, not only will the mountain of finance be unmovable but unable to mount as well. God gives us the tools we need to overcome these mountains and once we place kingdom principles in their proper places money problems that seem insurmountable before, become parts of our testimonies we share with others. We can all agree that unplanned expenses can happen. Life happens and throws monkey wrenches our way at all times, but by following these steps you become more prepared.

The truth of the matter is...money matters. Whether it matters a lot or a little to you; it matters. You find the mountain that much easier to conquer when you acknowledge just where money lines up on your list of priorities. God's desire is not for the mountain of finance to be one that terrifies you or prevents you from experiencing life the way He designed. Trust God's guidance and instruction to move or climb the mountain of finance in your life.

CHAPTER 3

RELATIONAL MOUNTAINS
CONTRIBUTED BY: GABRIELLE CRUMP

"The quality of your life is the quality of your relationships."
- Tony Robbins

Humans are said to possess a fundamental need to develop and maintain at least a small amount of long-term, affirmative, and significant interpersonal relationships. Throughout our lives, we find that this innate desire plays a major role in our optimism about the lives we live. From the moment a child is born into this world they crave the attention of and connection with their mother and father. As time goes on friendships are formed that help shape who we become. Along with friendships are more intimate, personal relationships, and the first signs of budding love sets the tone for the citizens we will one day become. And let's not forget one of the most life-changing and important relationships anyone can have...the significant relationship with the Creator of heaven and earth. So what happens when these relationships are not fully developed the way they ought to be; or those relationships that are not developed at all? It's a known fact that certain relationships shape the way we relate to the world and others around us. So what happens when a frayed relationship with one or multiple primary factors become mountains far too high and too wide to climb?

MATERNAL STRAINS

One of the earliest and most significant relationships in a person's life is the relationship between a child and his or her mother. From the moment God conceives us in our mothers' wombs, the relationship is established. Truthfully, a mother's response to her pregnancy plays such a pivotal role in the outcome of the immediate relationship with the child. Children who are adopted may feel a sense of rejection at some point in their lives when they learn of the truth. But it's not just children who are orphaned, adopted, or even fostered who experience a mountain of rejection and neglect from their mothers. Many children who live with their biological mothers, especially as primary caregivers, encounter a similar mountain in life. Why? Because, when the relationship between mother and child is built on mistrust, anger, regret and no Christ-like foundation, many mothers and children spend years affected by a mountain of relational defeat. No daughter (or son for that matter) wants to spend a lifetime feeling as if she has no hope for a healthy relationship with her mother. But the truth is, many do. So many women fall into the generational curse of having children before they are emotionally, mentally, financially, and/or physically prepared to bring one into the world. Consider the 16-year-old who has just found out she is expecting a child with the love of her life, "Mr. Right" who is just as ill-prepared and ill equipped as she is. Although he may have a promising future ahead of him, he's no more prepared for the commitment of a child than the young girl who, ironically enough, has no mother figure in her life. The mountain of maternal strains has already formed in her own life, how can she possibly overcome the same obstacle in her child's life?

Requesting the help of those around her including family and family friends, she begins her journey to raise their child, a daughter, the best way she knows how. As time passes and the young mother grows older, she begins to realize just how much being a teen mom has cost her. She never imagined her freedom to come and go as she pleases would become a distant dream of her past, her youthful years. It is then that she determines it will no longer limit her. She begins to pursue careers, school, and for the sake of her sanity relationships with men who can take her mind off being a mother.

She travels the world and jet sets with old friends, all while back home her daughter's mountain of maternal strain grows bigger and wider. People that the mother feels as though she can trust violate the daughter. The daughter spirals into a life consistent with pain, feelings of rejection, bad choices, and pure sadness. How does the mother come to recognize that the priorities she's chosen have not benefited her or her daughter? How does the daughter regain the trust in her mother? How do mother and daughter reconcile back to a healthy and functioning relationship?

Christ makes all the difference. For both mother and child, when a strained relationship becomes Mt. Kilimanjaro, the only factor possible to consider mending this brokenness is Christ Himself. Jesus is the perfect teacher of love, forgiveness and wholeness. Without Him, the mother holds on to regret, unforgiveness, and anger. Without Him the daughter holds on to rejection, resentment, and anger towards those who abused her. God's word tells us that with Christ all things are possible. This does not just include the job or career we seek, the dream of marriage and family. "All things" truly means **ALL THINGS**, including freedom from the mountains of your past.

The mountain of maternal strains, is one all too familiar mountain for many nonbelievers and believers alike. It's important to know that you can and WILL move the mountain of maternal strain in your life and have a functional God-centered mother/daughter relationship. You may be the mother who neglected her child(ren), in order to pursue careers, men, or your independence. Or you may be the daughter who suffered abuse at the hand of someone else, or simply feel as if you were not afforded the opportunity to grow with your mother the way you felt necessary. There is help and there is hope and His name is Jesus Christ.

*[Dear Heavenly Father, thank you that I now realize my mountains are only keeping me from fulfilling my true purpose in you! The mountain of maternal strains has kept me from being the Godly (mother/daughter) you purposed me to be and I surrender myself and this mountain to you. I give you my feelings of regret, rejection, anger, sadness, fear, and low self-worth. I give you my pain, my doubts, and my resentment towards all of those who have hurt me and I ask you to heal me and to lead me in a passionate walk of forgiveness. I pray that you would give me the strength to pursue a life that pleases you forgiving those who caused me years of hurt. And most of all I ask that You would help me to forgive myself. I thank you that **THIS** mountain has been moved, never to form again! In Christ Jesus' name, Amen.]*

PATERNAL ABSENCE

So, maybe your mountain isn't that of maternal strains. Maybe you had a mother in your life that placed you as priority in her life and ensured you knew just how important you were to her. Maybe you are like many others who associate the mountain in their lives with that of a different parental absence. Maybe your mountain is the mountain of paternal absence!

It's on every famous TV show, in almost every book, and in every newspaper article. "The effects of a father's absence in the home..." The father leaves the mother or is never present to begin with and the child spirals out of control. Children who grow up without fathers are more likely to abuse drugs, sex, money, etc. I know from personal experience, just how damaging the effects can be from a father not "stepping up to the plate" in terms of his parental duties.

I suffered years from mountains of rejection, identity issues, and poor decision making due in part to my biological father's failure to deliver on SO many promises. Even with my new God-given father through marriage in the picture, things were not the same and as a child I was well aware of the differences between my two father figures. On one hand the father God had blessed me with who married my mother was always supportive, always encouraging, and always reassuring. My biological father however, was the total opposite. He never kept his word, never made me feel like I mattered in his life, and always put others before me. These issues don't go over well in the mind of any child who feels as if the one person who should offer validation in their lives is not even thinking about how their life decisions are affecting the child they helped create.

Growing up with the towering mountain of paternal absence comes at cost far too high for any child to pay. I can remember times where I'd pray that God would just "help my daddy love me." Love me the way he loved my two older brothers. Love me the way he loved the various women he'd dated over the years. And love me the way he loved sports, grilling, and hunting. For any child this could cause damaging repercussions. It wasn't until my 16th birthday that God released me from the mountain of paternal absence that freed me to love Him (God), myself, and those closest to me, the way it had always been intended. God had to reveal Himself to me in a way only He could. Sure my father had failed to "man-up" and be the father he needed to be. Sure I'd lost sight of who I was and who I wanted to be early in life because I didn't have the stability from my biological father that I felt I deserved. But could I continue to use that as the reason I continued down a path of self-doubt and emotional defeat? Many things took place while I was under the supposed care of my biological father and instead of owning up to the fact that he was not as present as he should have been he shifted blame and made me regret the day I was born. I hated myself because my biological father refused to love me the way any and all children deserve to be loved. It took so much time for me to really begin to love and see myself the way God loved and saw me.

God spoke and said that I could no longer blame my biological father, be angry with him, or even fault the women in his life for not holding him more accountable. It was up to me to forgive this man for things he did or didn't do. But no only did I have to forgive him. I had to ask God to forgive me. For blaming Him for the choices my biological father made. I had to seek God to forgive me for being angry and for lashing out and acting out against those who had always been there for me. You often here the cliché "forgiveness isn't for the other person it's for you." And no words had ever rung more true than these the day I finally decided that I would not allow this mountain to follow me into my adult years. Of course I still made bad choices and didn't always feel as secure with myself all the time. But my biological father no longer had the power over me that he once did. It was not until I forgave my biological father in my heart that I was able to love and appreciate my Father in heaven and my earthly father God had blessed me with. I even went as far as calling a family meeting with everyone I felt played an intricate role in my childhood and discussed the mountain that had formed in my life and publicly announced my forgiveness. My biological father's ways never changed. He continued to deny certain things, lie about certain things, and break promises. Well into my early twenties he refused to admit to and acknowledge many things that occurred over the course of time, but it didn't matter anymore. I had found my peace and there was nothing anyone or anything could do to take that from me.

Paternal absence doesn't just occur when a father is out of the picture completely, or semi in the picture. Sometimes it happens when your biological father is physically in the home with you but is not spiritually and/or emotionally there for you. Many times fathers are in the home but so many other things take precedence over the children they've helped bring into the world. Be it careers, money, hobbies, and on and on. It's important to take a step back and acknowledge the affect this mountain is having in your life. You will continue to make bad choices, not feel whole, not pursue purpose, and blame God and others, for your life choices until you acknowledge and seek God's guidance on how to forgive and move the mountain of paternal absence in your life. Without Christ there again is no means of healing. Fathers and their children can have healthy, functioning, God centered relationships. If you're a father who has neglected to be who he needed to be in the life of your child, God offers forgiveness to you and it's never too late to be who He designed you to be. Maybe you're the child who feels as if you were neglected and because of that failed to make the best choices in life, God offers you healing, but that healing starts with your willingness to forgive. You can be free and you deserve to be free.

[Dear Heavenly Father, thank you for helping me to acknowledge the mountain of paternal absence and the affects it has caused in my life. God please forgive me for any anger I've had against you, myself, my father, and those close to me. I ask right now that you would begin the healing process. I realize that it begins with my willingness to forgive and I sincerely forgive myself/my father for the paternal absence mountain. Remove the feelings of low self-esteem, anger, rejection, fear, doubt, and resentment, and help me to walk in the fullness of who you are in my life. Thank you for being the father to me that I've always deserved. Thank you for loving me so much that you sent your only Son to die for me. Help me to live with a passion to forgive that I may pursue my purpose and live a fulfilled life with you and for you. In Christ Jesus' name, amen.]

IRRECONCILABLE DIFFERENCES

Significant relationships don't just begin and end with our parents, although the relationship with our parents plays a huge role in the outcome of the relationship we are going to discuss in this category. Sometimes the relational mountain in our life happens to be the one we promised to commit to for the rest of our lives... our significant other! When you read about or hear a couple's testimony on the number one reason they decided to seek a divorce a majority of them would say: irreconcilable differences. What are irreconcilable differences and why do they affect so many couples? Especially Christian couples? How can the mountain of irreconcilable differences be moved so that your marriage can be taken back and together you and your mate can win in the battle against your marriage? How can you find the love and passion to believe in the vow "until death do us apart" once again?

Irreconcilable differences are defined as "the existence of significant differences between a married couple that are so great and beyond resolution as to make the marriage unworkable". And for many couples this is primary means for divorce. What can happen in a marriage so damaging as to make one or both people feel as if their marriage is beyond repair? Well, many things can contribute to feeling this way: money, sexual issues, children/parenting, and many other things. However, many Christian couples forget the God-factor. A marriage may become too much for one or even both persons to bear, but nothing is ever too great for God, including the mountain of irreconcilable differences within your marriage.

God desires to have husband and wife live in holy matrimony the way He purposed it from the very beginning. However too many couples let too many other factors dictate the course of their marriage rather than the one who wrote the blueprint for it, God. Men and women get married and continue living as if they were dating. Socializing and living on a whim instead of praying with their mates and really finding out what the plan is for the marital relationship. Friends, single or married, become distractions. Money becomes a motivator for some and a sore spot for others. And when children are brought into the picture the dynamics that used to place one person as a priority, slowly begin to diminish. And many feel as if these seemingly "small" issues contribute to infidelity in marriage. But I see it otherwise. Husbands and wives don't commit adultery because they don't know how to commit to their mate. They commit adultery because they don't know how and won't commit to God.

The mountain of irreconcilable differences grows with every grueling argument and inconsiderate act of emotion. Many couples find that the statement of "no divorce" sounds good up until the point where you can no longer accept the fact that the one thing you thought you'd be able to live through when it happened to others, happens to you. For every couple this one thing could be different. One couple's last straw could be infidelity; another's could be an addiction to drugs, pornography, or gambling. And for another couple it could be not being placed as the proper priority in the life of the spouse. Whatever the mountain may be that has caused you to question the duration of your marriage, you have to view it as a mountain, and mountains were made to be moved! And God, through His word, has given us the tools we need to speak to the mountain of irreconcilable differences and demand it to move. No the pain from what a spouse has done or is doing does not heal overnight, but if you still believe in your marriage and have a hope in your God, there is no deed, no circumstance, no situation too hard for God to handle. Communicate with your spouse about the mountain that has driven you to the point where divorce seems like the only way out. Seek God on the necessary steps that need to be taken to go from a broken state back to a whole state. God desires to see the mountain of irreconcilable difference mounted and moved and you and your mate living in purpose together.

It's often expressed that the first year of marriage is the hardest, and during that year it seems like the devil gives you every reason under the sun to want to bail out. But the truth is, every year is just as hard as the first, and it's up to you and your spouse to place God as the head of your home and marriage in order to make the hard times seem like walks in the park. It is possible to live peaceable within your marriage. It is possible to love and enjoy your marriage the way you once did. The only thing you have to do is submit to God's way of doing things. Loving your spouse, the way God loves you, forgiving your spouse freely and often just as God forgives you freely and often and refusing to let anything or anyone come in between that love. The mountain of irreconcilable differences will only hinder you as long as you give it the power to do so. Your freedom from pain, hurt, guilt, and defeat within marriage is found in four simple words: "Help me to forgive." Learn to forgive and watch your marital mountains become testimonies that enrich the lives of others all around.

[Dear Heavenly Father, help me to forgive. Help me to forgive myself for not placing you where you belonged in my marriage. Help me to forgive my spouse for the pain they have caused me and the hurt I continue to feel. Help me to see the beauty in forgiveness and to remember Mark 10:9 which declares that what You have joined together let no one separate. Thank you for forgiving me that I may forgive others. Thank you that as I seek to forgive my spouse I will not hold on to their faults as tools of hurt but that a healing process for the both of us would begin and we would pursue purpose within our marriage together under your divine leadership and instruction. In Christ Jesus' name, Amen]

Forgiving a person does not mean that the relationship is rekindled and that two people become the best of friends.

Sometimes forgiveness simply means you no longer have control in my life. Because sometimes circumstances prevent us from being able to be in full fellowship with the other person and that's okay! God wants us to see the importance in forgiving, the freedom in forgiving, and the peace in forgiving. His love was shown through His sacrifice of Jesus Christ and it was the ultimate sacrifice. God wants us to see Him as the father in heaven who loves us beyond our faults and beyond our doubts and beyond our fears. He doesn't want us to see Him as a distant God who is not concerned with our internal affairs. He wants us to know, trust and believe that Matthew 21:21 can be true of any mountain in our lives; maternal strains, paternal absence, or marital matters. He desires to help us move the relational mountains that deplete and distract us from fulfilling our purposes here on earth. Each of these mountains has a far greater effect on the most important relationship we will ever have; and that's the one between us and our heavenly Father. If we don't move these mountains and overcome them our relationship with God suffers dramatically. It's up to you to seek the peace and the healing you need to move the relational mountains in your life.

CHAPTER 4

RELIGIOUS MOUNTAINS

"Choose Your Friends with Caution, Plan Your Future with Purpose, Frame Your Life with Faith" - Thomas S. Monson

A great number of believers readily identify with "religion" as opposed to spiritual relationship. It's somewhat ironic because many experience it in similar ways but in different stages of their lives. Mountains of religion manifest in various forms. This religious conundrum is one of epic proportions that produces doubt and questionable faith to the challenge of believing that "gathering together with likeminded individuals" is really a benefit. For me, spiritual mountains came in three very life changing experiences that eventually paved the way for the platform on which I stand today.

Spiritual or religious mountains may seem like they are the end of your world of faith, but in all actuality they can be the conduits that thrust you into the spiritual person you were destined to be. In order to overcome religious mountains in life, one must first be both willing and committed to acknowledge the area in which the issue has formed. A significant number of novice and seasoned believers alike find themselves facing religious mountains; however, instead of identifying and confronting them in faith, the mountains overwhelm them and instills so much fear that not only does their faith falter but their relationship with Jesus suffers.

Religious mountains, once formed, are resistant to being moved. Religious mountains resemble spirituality in that the Bible text is often referenced but seldom practiced. Religious mountains cross all spiritual and Biblical boundaries. The Bible states, in part, "For God is Spirit, so those who worship him must worship in spirit and in truth." One cannot display behaviors similar to that of the Pharisees while professing life as that of the Holy Savior. I'm often perplexed by this seemingly normal yet cavalier attitude. This "religious" attitude is accepted more than we'd like to admit.

It would have been so easy for me to assimilate and never accept Christ fully...through deliberate actions of spiritual awareness and discipline. I liken religious mountains to generational curses. Typically speaking, parents set both the paradigm and the tone for their child(ren)'s spiritual/religious views. It's so liberating to break free of religious mountains. I'd sit and watch those closest to me (my mother) talk Godly, sing weekly, and attend service "religiously". I never really focused on others and their lifestyles. I believed it was my parents' responsibility to guide me in this area! Some of you may take offense to my frankness on this spiritual quagmire, especially since I've elected to reference my mother. Don't be offended; but rather, evaluate your relationship with God and your example to others who may look to you for guidance. Are you more religious or spiritual? Do you follow rules the way you choose and condemn others who fall beneath your ideals or standards? Proceed with caution, a religious mountain may be forming.

Still others would erroneously assume that the experience was fruitless or unproductive. Those individuals would be so wrong! I learned a great deal from the experience, some painful and some impactful but all beneficial. You'll notice that Romans 8:28 is one of my absolute favorite scriptures! I learned how to trust Jehovah for my God given "Me-nistry". The book of Romans describes the love God deposited in us prior to birth. It was during my difficult transitional period that I realized there was more for me and more to me than I'd actually recognized. It's a life defining moment when you come to the realization that where you are presently, is not as good as it gets!

Religious mountains don't have to invade your life! You possess the authority to move it! Once you recognize it; move it! Religious mountains prohibit us from tapping in to our various gifts and talents; our "Me-nistries". Religious mountains also impede our spiritual growth. So, respond expeditiously and act immediately! I ultimately chose to live a life of holiness rather than hypocrisy, a life of fulfillment rather than regret, a life of purpose as opposed to chaos. I'm not the only one who has conquered this mountain, many others have also!

BEYOND THE HURT

One very familiar mountain that both recent and experienced believers endure is the mountain of hurt within the church. This mountain affects more than just a believer's ability to sympathize within the church and with other believers but it pushes them further away from Gods truth. I faced hurt within the church very early in my life. I always knew that there was something uniquely creative yet bold about me! Even after the abuse I'd faced as a young child, I recognized God's favor both in and on my life. His hands were upon my life and He had gifted me to sympathize with the spirits of various people. Nevertheless, just as much as I could recognize this amidst my [personal] dysfunction, it was my conclusion that those within the church recognized it, yet remained silent. They did not possess the courage to speak up or out. It was more convenient for many of them to sit quietly and discuss my dysfunction with one another. Has this ever happened to you? I can vividly remember my own mother sharing parts of my personal life within the church, not in a way as to seek support or help, but to divert attention from herself and her own sins and struggles. Instead of those in the church seeing a hurt young girl and coming together to receive her in love, they saw an opportunity to judge and lie and abuse authority.

Although it's been more than twenty years since my initial encounter and eventual revelation of authentic forgiveness through faith in Christ's love, I see some of the same issues facing today's millennials. It's not surprising that many young believers today experience the same realities within the four church walls and, that's disheartening. Instead of seeing hurting individuals as Jesus saw people, with love and hopeful sincerity, many of today's "church people" see individuals as an opportunity to judge and ridicule without full knowledge of who that person is and what it is they're facing or have endured.

Jesus instructs believers to respond in love. But what we witness in churches today is a significant number of individuals with a false sense of self and no love for those around them. The early church in the book of Acts focused on this principle concept; love. Acts 2:45 instructs us how they sold possessions to give to those among them in need, what a beautiful example. Imagine how much more the church would grow and how much faster Christianity "the faith" would expand if all churches responded to the need of others and not the selfish desires of themselves.

Maybe you were the promiscuous teen (I was) who was ostracized in a church and vowed to never again set foot in a church. Maybe you were the young adult who struggled with sexual identity and, instead of being welcomed with love and compassion, you were rejected and judged by the members and leaders. The mountains are real! They are consequential and, often times overwhelming. Additionally, the mountains may negatively influence the way new converts perceive Christ and His authority over mountains! It's incumbent upon us to demonstrate strength, valor, and faith during our mountain moving encounters. Question, have you ever felt so intimidated by your mountains that you chose to ignore the mountain instead of confront it?

In order to move the "religion" mountain (of hurt within the church) we must not only be able to identify the issue that has surfaced but also be willing to effectively conquer It. This life application becomes one of the most difficult components of moving the mountain because it requires you returning to the place in which you experienced the hurt; not only from an emotional aspect but a psychological one as well.

EMOTIONALLY

One may have to return to painful feelings, suppressed over time. Feelings you may have worked on years and years to forget, but revisiting those raw emotions allows others to understand better. It's vital that when recounting these issues, you remember not to respond in a way that causes more damage. God's word informs us that it's okay to be angry but not to react to that anger with sin (Eph.4:26).

It's important to identify the branches that lie at the root of the issue. Was it those painful feelings of rejection, the feelings of betrayal, the feelings of defeat that stemmed from this initial hurt that caused you to become angry with not only the church but God as well? Acknowledging these branches helps you and others to better understand the situation and makes for a better healing process.

Not only do we have to revisit emotions, but we must also revisit the physical and psychological aspects of the hurt as well. This may include a particular ministry or ministries and the individual(s) who offended you. The word of God instructs us to go to our brother/sister if they have sinned against You (Matt 18:15-17). God doesn't just place that in the bible for a good read but He intends for us to practice it. In order to move the mountain of hurt faced within the "church", one must be willing to return to those people or that person who caused the offense. Maybe it's returning to the church and talking with the Pastor.

As an ordained minister, I can attest to the fact that many pastors embrace the opportunity to reconcile broken relationships that may have occurred under their leadership. Maybe that means you have to go and speak with specific individuals within the church and humbly, yet unapologetically inform them that they offended you, hurt you, caused you to experience doubt in yourself and in the church and ultimately in God. This may be difficult and may require a mediator depending on the depth of the offense. However, there will be a true sense of peace and a true burden lifted when you are able to face this mountain both figuratively and literally.

If you're unsure whether or not you are facing a mountain that stems from hurt within the church consider the following to help you determine: How do you respond to the idea of church? How is your attitude toward Christian individuals? How are your feelings toward the Christian faith? Do you generalize all Christians? Are church doors off limits because you feel "Christians are worse than secular individuals"? If you are a "church-goer", do you prefer larger ministries where you can get lost in the crowd or don't have to be in the "religious spotlight"? Your response to these questions reveals a lot about whether or not you are currently facing the spiritual mountain of "church hurt".

God's intended design for those who consider themselves Christians, was neither wrapped in arrogance nor self-righteousness, but rather lovingkindness, gentleness, meekness, and long suffering (to name a few) like Jesus was. Jesus didn't judge those who weren't "perfect", those who had fallen, those who had lost their way. Instead, He met them where they were; offered His love, His care and, ultimately, surrendered His life, but not only for those who were willing to admit they were broken, but also the ones who thought they were fixed but in much distress spiritually. When you've been hurt within the church or by someone who was thought to be a Christ-follower, the damage is indeed great and the mountain is big, but the damage is not irreparable, and the mountain is never too great to be moved.

Breaking Tradition

The next spiritual mountain believers encounter at any given point in their walk with God is the mountain of traditionalism. Traditionalism in religion occurs when the relationship aspect of a Christ-centered life is eclipsed by legalism and self-righteousness. The proverbial "great debate" involves religion vs relationship and the manner in which one lives determines the degree to which the mountain of tradition has influenced you.

In recent years, the battle over whose denomination is more accurate has become more problematic than in previous years (another distraction). When life becomes more about doing good according to others' standards, looking prominent, saying the right things, but not living the life one professes while simultaneously avoiding the "root", one can almost assuredly say that traditionalism has invaded his or her life. I can remember attending ministries where I was expected to dress, speak, and live in accordance with scripture in order to be perceived a certain way. However, in the same instance, one could be living the total opposite of what she was presumed to be living.

Jesus never instructs His disciples to look a certain way, but always compelled them to allow their lives to exemplify one that represents a love for God. Traditionalism prevents one from experiencing the true beauty of God's grace and forgiveness. Traditionalism encompasses legalism with extreme traces of religion. Consider the woman caught in the act of adultery. Religious leaders scowled her and religious practices called for her to be killed, but relationship with Christ called for grace.

[Authentic] Relationships challenge us to respond with forgiveness, love, and grace in every situation. As unthreatening as the mountain of traditionalism may sound, it causes more damage to our long term walk of faith than many realize. Traditionalism seals us in a state of bondage to people and rules we are incapable of following perfectly while Godly relationship encourages us to live in the freedom God offers through Christ's perfect life.

When your life is tradition based, prayer becomes more about fancy talk and flattering words than about a pouring out of our hearts to the Father's throne. If you find yourself anxious and always zealous to pray among crowds but very seldom praying in your own quiet prayer closet, you may be experiencing the mountain of traditionalism. And, if those prayers are followed by overthinking the prayers, the mountain of traditionalism may be one that needs to be moved immediately. "Did I sound right?" "Did I say the right things?" "Did I use enough elaborate scriptures?" The aforementioned are all examples of questions you may find yourself asking, if you are facing this particular mountain. Prayer should always be about the beauty and liberty of simply talking with You Heavenly Father. Matthew 6:5 encourages us not to pray as the hypocrites pray, seeking applause from man and not with sincere hearts to God.

Nonetheless, the "traditionalism" mountain can be moved by repenting and asking God to transform one's heart and open one's eyes to see Him and your walk with Him as an opportunity to grow while simultaneously embracing a lifelong relationship that includes consistent communication. Additionally, a believer must be willing to commit to a change in the way he or she views Christianity. The focus is "relationship" as opposed to "religion". The Pharisees' traditional dogma challenged the very essence of Christ. It's imperative that believers impose relationship in lieu of religion. Jesus challenged the Pharisees in many New Testament scriptures.

Regular church attendance and fellowship is not only God ordained, but also spiritually beneficial in areas of accountability and growth. Religious mindsets prove difficult to overcome and even more difficult to implement. It is incumbent upon the believer to renounce the power of traditional thinking hovering over your life as not to distort the truth of the gospel and the way in which God intends to reach those all over the world. Traditional thinking and living affects one's effectiveness in ministry. It affects the way you view yourself and the way you view others. It also affects the way you pursue the purpose in which you are supposed to live for God, and that is reaching those who don't know who Jesus Christ is. Traditions are good in their proper places, like Christmas and family traditions, but when it comes to a walk with God traditionalism should never be an issue. Relationship and religion are two distinctively different perspectives in relation to God and the Christian walk. Don't allow the "mountain of traditionalism" to prevent you from fulfilling your God given purpose in this life.

BELIEVING IN THE ME-NISTRY

The final spiritual mountain is the faith vs fear factor. Have you ever considered how easy it is to live in the shadow of someone else instead of stepping out to pursue your destiny? Consider this, have you ever felt as if you knew God Himself had called you to do more than what you were currently doing? To be more than what you currently were? To step out of your comfort zone and into the battlefield? How do you go from sitting on the bench of fear into the purpose of "who" God called you to be, if fear exists between you and the initial step? The mountain of fear concerns many believers. I say this because it concerned me for quite some time. "How can I afford to..." "How will they respond..." "What if it doesn't..." Are all questions that perplex our minds. Looking up at the peak of the mountain of fear can cause a spirit of intimidation and the inability to step out into the ministry God placed in our hearts before we were even birthed into existence. For me, conquering the mountain of fear in regard to my ME-nistry was one I was determined to defeat...to conquer, to move!

When we ignore the promptings of God's Spirit compelling us to step out [in faith] and begin truly operating in purpose, we not only delay fulfilling purpose, but we may also contribute to someone else's fear concerning their Me-nistry. From a very young age, I knew God had prepared and positioned me for ministry with young girls and women; particularly those suffering and recovering from various types of abuse. Had I allowed the mountain of unbelief in my Me-nistry to continue to overwhelm and torment me, I never would have stepped into my promised place of purpose. Question, are you prepared to press toward the mark of the prize of the high calling in Christ Jesus?

Having the faith, courage, and determination to trust [in God] to step out and establish a church, a Christian academy, and a women's ministry was not easy. The cynics continued whispering words of doubt silently awaiting my failure. Glory! Many of whom were my family members. They aborted the mission while I was planning. Even my biological parents, whom I thought would be most excited for me, allowed their personal doubts, fears and lack of fulfillment to cause them to speak against what I knew God had spoken to me to do. As much as it hurt me to hear the words while experiencing their lack of support and encouragement, it didn't force me to falter under the false power of the "religious" mountain. It hurt, but the hurt challenged me to increase my trust in Jehovah's promises! I endured many long days and even longer nights; however, I never relented. I risked so much and sacrificed even more to pursue what God had birthed into my spirit because I was determined to see His will fulfilled in my life, that I might be an example to other [women] who were afraid to step out on faith and trust God.

I'm certain that you've experienced mountains that caused your knees to buckle, your heart to race and, your faith to waiver! Glory be to our God for strengthening us in our times of weakness! Remember this, we are overcomers! We are victorious because He causes us to triumph! And, like our Savior, Jesus Christ, we recognize mountains as distractions, hindrances, or challenges that we have the power to overcome by faith. Matthew 21:21 provides specific instructions [to the believer] concerning the art of mountain moving. I'm encouraged to challenge you to face the mountains in your life. The mountain is not greater than you!

These are the realities many believers experience. God has afforded us our very own area of ministry. Your ministry may not be mine, standing and speaking before crowds, authoring books, or hosting conferences for women. Maybe your ministry is working with children and babies in your local church, feeding the homeless, volunteering your time with the elderly or widowed. Whatever your ME-nistry is, the longer the mountain of fear and doubt linger in your life, the longer your passion is delayed. Remember, there are individuals waiting to experience your God given ME-nistry!

Satan capitalizes on the fears and self-doubt to not only keep us from believing in our ME-nistry but also to prevent us from believing and trusting in God. Matthew 19:26 tells us that with man things are impossible but with God nothing is impossible. That's no cliché, that's no cute maxim. It's a foundational truth you must have in order to move the mountain of self-doubt in your ME-nistry. God wouldn't have given it to you if He didn't know you could take it on. Don't allow this spiritual mountain to keep you bound to a life of sadness, frustration, and unfulfillment.

Someone needs to hear your testimony! Someone needs to feel the warmth of your hug or the soothing sound of your voice. Every "born again" believer possesses a ME-nistry within us just waiting for us to move the mountain of fear that we may be able to pursue it passionately with full trust that God will provide us with the resources, support and network we need to accomplish His will.

CHAPTER 5

IDENTITY MOUNTAINS
CONTRIBUTED BY: GABRIELLE CRUMP

"The degree to which a person can grow is directly proportional to the amount of truth he can accept about himself without running away."- Leland Val Van de Wall

Who am I? And why am I here? Are two of the biggest posed questions by men, women, and children. The internal longing to find out who you are and what your purpose is for being here on earth is one challenging mountain individuals encounter at various points in their lives. There's no wonder why so many people are attempting to find out "who they want to be when they grow up" well into adulthood. So what do you do when you find yourself at the crossroads? How do you overcome the mountain of identity crisis and not allow it to plague your future endeavors? And how does God play a role in helping you determine just why you're here?

GUESS WHO

The mountain of identity crisis can be one that stumps the wealthiest person to the same degree in which it puzzles the "average Joe". The first step we need to take in moving the mountain of identity issues within our lives is recognizing the two key factors in our lives that ultimately influence who we become. Finding out your true identity can (a lot of times) seem like you're playing a round of the game of Guess Who. In the game of "Guess Who" you sit across from an opponent and ask yes and no descriptive questions attempting to guess who the name of the person they have. In our case, we are seeking our own names and who you ask plays just as important a role as what you ask.

IDENTITY THIEF

When you don't know who you are and why you're here, you spend a lot of time in search of what you like. What fits me? What intrigues me? What motivates me? These are all great questions, but again who you ask can affect if the mountain of identity crisis grows or becomes smaller. A relationship with God is so beneficial in finding out who you are for so many reasons. The first reason is it lowers your chances of being a victim of identity theft. Identity theft is when one person uses another person's private identifying information. Spending years in same-sex relationships, abusive relationships, fornication, adultery, so on and so forth, are all examples of the identity thief's that creep into our lives and cause us to lose precious time being in purpose and enjoying the God given life we deserve. Satan is the puppeteer behind the scenes of the identity theft plot. He uses these tactics to distract and destroy our purposes and identities before we even have the opportunity to know what they are.

Why does child sexual abuse spate so many families worldwide? It's because Satan, the greatest identity thief of all times, uses these traumatic experiences to infiltrate the hearts and minds of people while they are children. Satan knows that if he can have us in a state of identity crisis beginning in our childhood, we have a far greater chance (without Christ) of wasting years unsure of who we are and living less than holy lifestyles. Homosexuality, fornication, drug and alcohol abuse, all stem from a lack of knowing who we are. They all lead to us being out of fellowship with our Heavenly Father. When we realize that there is an identity thief on the loose we take the necessary precautions to protect our identity. We have all heard the stories and seen the movies about what happens when your identity is stolen. The stories shake us so much that we take extra steps to prevent it from happening to us. We make purchases and go to some very extreme measures to ensure the safety of our identity because no one in their right mind wants to be a victim of identity theft. We teach our children the importance of keeping personal and private matters, personal and private. And we set up back up plans for our back up plans in case anything goes wrong. So if we take such measures to protect our physical identities, why wouldn't we do the same, if not more to protect our spiritual identities?

Instead of spending time around the dinner table talking about the stock market and 5-year career goals, why don't we spend time communicating the importance of developing a strong, reliable, unwavering relationship with God? Why don't we spend more time reading our bibles and talking to

God about really finding out why certain things happened in our lives and what the next steps are in fulfilling our purpose? It's because whatever Satan can do to keep you from focusing on your spiritual identity; he will do, so that he can build up just enough information to steal what's most valuable to you...who you are.

LifeLock

When your identity is in question or has been outright stolen, you take the necessary steps to get your identity back where it was before the thief wreaked havoc. The same stands for your spiritual identity. When Satan, the adversary, has stolen your spiritual identity it's up to you to regain your spiritual value by getting the insurance and assurance from the only person who can provide it, Jesus Christ. The mountain of identity crisis can peak at any given time in your life. You may not even notice the subtle signs that the mountain is growing until that one morning you wake up and look in the mirror and no longer recognize the reflection you see. Maybe it's the hangover hair and the sleeping body resting in your bed from the one-night stand. Maybe it's the black eye and swollen lip from the punches you endured the night before. Maybe it's the fact that no matter how many physical changes you've made to your body your heart still flutters from the truth that you're NOT the man you've doctored yourself up to be, but still the girl He created you to be. Whatever the reason, you see that something is wrong and you finally decide that enough is enough.

Jesus came to earth, lived life, and died just as you and I will do one day. But He didn't stay dead; He rose again with all glory and power in His hands. That's not some glorified make-believe fairytale, it's a true story with a beautiful message, that no matter what you've done how long you've done it, and how "wrong" you may think it is...Jesus died and rose again so that you could have hope in knowing that who you are today doesn't have to be who you are tomorrow, or even better, five minutes from now. Jesus lived a perfect life and Satan still tried to steal His identity, and though he tried as hard as he could, like the big bad wolf, he was unsuccessful. And he can be unsuccessful in his pursuit to steal, or continue to steal, your spiritual identity. God offers us a way of escape and a surefire way to overcome this tall and wide mountain in our lives and that is by accepting His Son Jesus as our Lord and Savior. When you accept Jesus AND put Him in His rightful place in your life, the discovery of who you are and who you are destined to be, become that much easier to identify. It never ceases to amaze me how many people testify to finding out their gifts and talents and their strengths when they give Christ a chance.

I can remember spending years of my childhood hating who I was. I spent so many nights asking God angrily, why He'd allowed me to be born and why he wouldn't just let me die. As I grew up I continue to battle with emotional issues. School didn't make it better because as we all know, a majority of school years are spent finding a clique and fitting in with the "in-crowd", for those outsiders struggling to relate this is often another snowball added to the top of an ever-growing mountain. Trying to define myself by other people's standards only proved to be ineffective. It was only when I had my epiphany with Jesus that I finally acknowledged the sin in my life and the mountain before me. There was only one thing left to do. Accept the journey and make the climb! But that's the beauty in allowing Jesus to be the "Life-coach" that helps you find out exactly who you are. He not only leads you step by step, but He makes the climb with you.

We can't allow Satan or any other person to determine who we are. People will abuse us, misuse us, tell us we won't amount to anything, but God comes in and says "For I know the plans I have for you, declares the Lord, plans for welfare and not for evil, to give you a future and a hope." And that hope He speaks of is in none other than Jesus. He desires to see us walking in the fullness of life. He desires to see us moving and overcoming the mountain of identity crisis in our lives. He has the golden step by step plan to taking back your life, the ultimate LifeLock, His word and His Son. When you factor in Jesus you not only find out who you are, you've taken a preventative measure in protecting who you are. When you are uncertain of who you are Satan can tempt you into believing you're someone else. But when God has signed your birth certificate, there's no questioning or denying who you are and Satan no longer poses a threat to the safety of that identity.

IDENTIFY THE ISSUES

Recognizing Satan's role in our mountain of identity crisis is important. Identifying God's role in moving the mountain is even more important. But let's be practical, you can't begin the process of discovery until you identify the issues that lead up to the crisis in the first place. One thing that's universally true regarding salvation is that you must first identify the fact that you need saving and that saving is from the sin that has kept you bound.

We all have different issues that cause us to have the identity issues in life we face. It could be the fact that we had an absent parent growing up. It could be that we were sexually abused as a child and that lead to a spirit of gender confusion.

It could be that we were physically abused as a child or watched a loved one being physically abused. Maybe for you it's losing someone who you thought you wouldn't be able to live without. Maybe it's low self-esteem and feelings of no self-worth that cause you to doubt your abilities. Or, acts of rebellion that lead to a disconnected relationship with God. Once you identify the issue or issues that contribute to the mountain of identity crisis you currently find yourself facing you are better equipped to cut it down at the root. Not only can you eradicate the root but it then becomes part of a powerful testimony used to motivate and encourage someone else to come out of the same or a similar identity crisis.

Think about how many people would be the victim of identity theft if others didn't share their stories. That's the amazing thing about encountering mountains. Once you've moved or mounted them, you get to rejoice in the victory with someone else. If mountain climbers trained for months at a time before they climbed the mountains around the world and lived to tell about it only not to tell, how discouraging would that be to someone who felt as if they wanted to conquer a mountain but couldn't simply because they'd never heard a success story. When we encounter our mountains and allow God to come in, heal us, and lead us in moving the mountain, we then have the responsibility to share that story and help inspire someone else to take the same step and enjoy the same freedom we do as mountain movers and overcomers of identity crisis.

Just like in the "Guess Who" game, the opponent's task is to keep you off the trail as long as possible so that you never figure out the name of the person they have. But when your opponent is God, He gives you the clues and hints you need to lead you to a sweet victory that lasts far longer than earthly means. It's eternal! When you know who you are and why you're here, your purpose goes far beyond a good career, a successful marriage, and a nice home. Knowing who you are means securing a home in eternity for your spirit. Heaven is a guaranteed expectance to those who trust in and identify with Jesus Christ and it makes all the difference in how you live each day on this earth.

[Dear Heavenly Father, thank you for helping me to identify the identity issues I have been facing all these years. Thank you for allowing me to have the opportunity to come to you, the one who created me, to find out who I really am and why you have placed me here. Thank you for Jesus and what He did for me on the cross. Thank you that I no longer allow Satan to use my spiritual identity to his advantage. Thank you that the identity issue of (CALL OUT YOUR SPECIFIC IDENTITY ISSUE) no longer towers over me paralyzing me with fear and insecurities. I repent of my sins and the anger I have held in my heart against you for the current status of my spiritual identification. I ask you to come into my heart and life and take charge of the matters in my life that influence who I am and who I am to become. I thank you for Jeremiah 29:11 and the life it speaks into my current situation. Help me to use the identity issues that have become great mountains in my life to encourage others to trust you to deliver them and move the mountain of Identity Crisis from their lives. Thank you for your love that covers a multitude if sin including any guilt I may have. Remove it and help me not to look back. In Christ Jesus' Name, Amen]

CHAPTER 6

DYSFUNCTIONAL
FAMILY MOUNTAINS
CONTRIBUTED BY: PAULA GEETER

"Dysfunctional families are the products of emotional dishonesty, [secrets], shame-based patriarchal society based upon beliefs that do not support loving self or loving [their] neighbors."
- Robert Burney

Dysfunctional family vs unfair family, can you identify them...

The family unit in today's society consists of most individuals attempting to recover from dysfunction or are currently living in it. The invitation is set for you to meet the Unfair Family in this reading. You may be able to recognize a few people in the family or even relate to them. The Unfair Family is a family where conflict, lying, pride, misbehaving, rebellion, abuse, neglect are just a few continual and regular practices in this group. Just reading the family's daily practices tell us that they are dysfunctional. They never tell about their dysfunction because of what others may think of them. Moreover, they try to hide themselves among the masses, but can quickly explode and send their toxic wastes of anger, hostility, jealousy, guilt, and pain down the mighty Mississippi River to hurt others when something doesn't go their way. The secrets of dysfunction are not exposed to those outside of the family. Dysfunction wears the best suits and dresses money can buy if possible when it is not among its kind, but the inside of dysfunction shows no love, no peace, no Jesus Christ. Individuals associated with dysfunctional families have unfulfilled lives because secrets of mental, physical, sexual or emotional torture do not permit them to move forward. So, they are stuck in the quick sand of personal deficiencies. What a legacy to leave your future generations – dysfunction, it is really unfair! If we could only fathom or imagine where we come from emotionally, mentally, physically and spiritually, it would give us a clear picture about where we are going in life. Are you dealing with dysfunction in your life?

Many individuals today deal with difficult or dysfunctional situations, parents, children, family, friends or even spouses on a daily basis. The hallmark of these difficult relationships is dysfunction. If difficult relationships were not dysfunctional, it wouldn't be so hard for us to handle it. These unhealthy relationships can make one's life a living hell. Moreover, it will affect your relationship with Jehovah, if you allow it.

Let us take a look at how an individual is affected by dysfunction. Well, in the Unfair family, we see the parents who are called "Victims" talking with one another while drinking alcohol and popping pills to medicate their pain of dysfunction from childhood. They believe consuming alcohol and drugs are ways to cope with their past issues and hurts. Now, there is a sister of one parent whose name is "Enabler". She loves to protect and take care of the problems the parents have raising their children. Enabler is the dependent because she does not experience the negative consequence of her actions. She is angry and resentful because she believes she has to take care of the family. Of course, Enabler has medical problems of her own such as hypertension, depression and diabetes because she is irresponsible about her own health needs due to thinking the family cannot survive without her. Hmmm, sounds familiar. Well, let me tell you about the children of the Unfair Family. Their names are Lost Child, Mascot, Family Hero and Scapegoat. The root of their dysfunction is sin from generational curses that have not been addressed. One may say that this is a Christian family who is well known in their church and pay their tithes and offering every Sunday. Well, just because we believe a person is saved through the acknowledgement of Jesus Christ in their heart that He was raised from the dead (Romans 10:9) does not mean they are free from dysfunction. Remember, there is a root cause to dysfunction. Let's get to the root of it!

A person can still become infected by their sin nature through being blinded by the truth of their family's dysfunction. Most people are broken individuals who are doing the best they can with what little they know. What if all a person knows is dysfunction? Difficult or dysfunctional people react to what they know, feel or believe. Of course, we all know that "hurt people, hurt people" is true. Since we know this statement, it does not give us the reason to excuse this behavior in our lives. Every individual has the right and responsibility to take care of herself and himself in the best way. Choosing to stay in a dysfunctional situation or family is not taking care of yourself. Staying in this disheartening situation is like living in a solitary confinement without parole. The best way is to walk away from the dysfunction. Ooh, this a hard thing to do if you've been involved for a long time because it is the only thing familiar to you. But God, can change any difficult or unhealthy situation into a healthy situation if one would only trust and obey His word and have an intimate relationship with Jesus Christ. If you looked at yourself in the mirror, would you see a healthy individual beyond your physical appearance? How healthy is your mind and heart, spiritually? Are you seeing pain, guilt, oppression, depression, rejection, defiance, hostility, insecurity, low self-esteem looking back at you? Do you live in a fantasy world where you are the only one in control and not God? Do you believe you have it all together without focusing on the real issues of why you are failing miserably in relationships, finances or even establishing a relationship with Jesus Christ? Dysfunction is serious...it attacks the mind and heart of an individual. One thing every one of us has to remember is that we can't choose our families and being in your particular family is unfair.

We tend to think of dysfunction as being a victim of an addiction – drugs, food, sex, physical and verbal abuse. However, these things are only the side effects of a dysfunction or better yet, the coping mechanisms to deal with dysfunction besides denial. Sometimes the root of dysfunction in our families is due to doing things our own way instead of God's way. We fall into sin because we neglect God's word or don't even have Jesus Christ as the center of our lives or in our mind. Look at it this way, the feelings of pain, insecurity, rejection, hatred and hostility are flowing in your family's spiritual blood line from thousands of years ago. When we don't deal with dysfunctions in our present life, it tends to encourage our children to live a life of rebellion, resistance, anger, defiant behaviors, blaming others and selfishness. Some children today are growing up in dysfunctional families not knowing who they are in Jesus Christ.

NAME THAT CHILD

Remember the names of the Unfair children – Lost Child, Hero, Scapegoat and Mascot. All these children have received the generational curses of their parents – Victims. Usually, each child may assume the role within the family to make up for the poor parenting. However, do children understand parenting skills? No, because they are children forming into adults. Hero, is the oldest child who is responsible for every one including her parents. She was pregnant by the age of 16 and is suffering from feelings of inadequacy and depression because she can't alone heal her family's wounds and be responsible for a newborn. She believes her dreams of a nursing career are unattainable. Hero feels isolated because she can't attend football games and cheerleading practices anymore because of her situation. Being the Hero in the family is tough because they are everything to everybody. Hero is the leader of the dysfunction, trying to have everything under control, but is missing out on his or her own spirituality. Here is the Lost Child, let me tell you about this individual. He is the outsider of the family because he feels he is being ignored by the parents because of their own issues. Lost Child is private, feels lonely and has poor communication skills. He is probably having some identity issues and confusion about who he is. If you know any Lost Children, they may drown their sorrows by overeating, alcohol or drug use, low self-esteem and often have few friends and find comfort in material possessions or animals. The Lost Child avoids seeking medical/psychiatric attention for their issues and remains isolative. Lawd, there are some lost children out there needing someone to pour spiritual knowledge into them about who they are in Jesus Christ so they can pursue their passion and possess hope. Unfair's child, Scapegoat acts with anger and defiance all the time, going to juvenile detention on the regular; however, Scapegoat is hurting so bad because the attention is not on him at all. He is a low performing student, disrespectful, hostile and irresponsible and has experienced many drugs and promiscuous sexual activity. He is in a gang and is involved with criminal activity in his neighborhood. He is labeled as the family's "problem child". Do you know any and why are they the "problem child"? Scapegoat does not understand that his defiant attitude may affect his future in having employment to earn adequate income. His cleverness and manipulative behaviors may even cause him to experience inauthentic and shallow relationships. He may have lost any spiritual potential or morality because of his rebellious nature. Well, there's Mascot, he is the clown of the family and hyperactive. He seeks attention from everybody...just annoying. He uses comedy to shield him from the problems of his family. He uses acting as a clown and immaturity to deal with problems to avoid running away. Mascot has a hard time concentrating on learning and fears looking honestly within himself to see his shortfalls. His hyperactivity is used as a way to cope instead of having a nervous breakdown. If his inner anxieties are not addressed, he may fall into a deeper mental illness and/or become chemically dependent or possibly suicidal. We, as adults, need to remember that children take on the parts of our roles which are usually the negative side. How do you think our children will have a life of vitality and fulfillment when they are messed up by our past because we fail to break the cycle of dysfunction? As adults, we can no longer hide the dysfunction in our family and let it transfuse poison into our children. Dysfunction is a crippling disease and it needs to be cut off immediately from the root for it to die!

On the website hopefortheheart.org, it has the illustration of the Unfair family, but it also describes their dysfunction as: "1) one where family members are impaired emotionally, psychologically and spiritually; 2) where improper and immature behaviors of at least one parent damages the growth of individuality and healthy relational skills among family members; 3) where everyone is negatively affected even when only family member experiences problems." In the Bible, Proverbs 11:29 (New Living Translation) mentions *"those who bring trouble on their families inherit the wind. The fool will be a servant to the wise"*. What are you bringing into your home or what are you allowing to be brought into your home?

Dysfunctional families, like the Unfair family, tend to be anxious. An example of this anxiety is child molestation or physical abuse that is a current cycle in the family. The victim of the abuse is told to keep it a secret or he or she may have told someone in the family of the molestation and/or abuse and the family member does not believe her or him. The person who is the victim becomes anxious because they are afraid of what will happen next or what they should do the next time it occurs. Anxiety in the dysfunctional family allows family members to talk about other family members ("I'm concerned that your mother is taking too many pain pills during the day") rather than directly talking to that individual. Dysfunctional family members take sides, love to divide the family, lose objectivity, love to control others who they believe are weaker than they are and focus on each other in a blaming way and then join other family member's campground to attack a family member physically, emotionally, or even spiritually. Ahh, Satan uses the closest thing or person to you to hurt you – family. When there is high anxiety in a difficult family, their reactions to situations are very loud and boisterous by what is said or done to fix or change a situation or another family member to be on their side. An example, "look what I did for you because you had nothing". This is where controlling behaviors arise in and take over. You can't change your family, but you can change yourself by changing your mindset, heart and motives to that of Jesus Christ.

You may have an unethical parent or grandparent, a sexually inappropriate aunt, uncle, sister, brother or cousin, a toxic mother or father in your family. These family members repeat destructive patterns for generations. It appears they drain the "fun" out of "dysfunctional". The first book of the Bible, Genesis (chapter 37), tells the story of a child who grew up in a dysfunctional family. Joseph was his name and he knew about jealousy, anger, dishonesty, vengefulness and fearfulness that passed down from one generation to the next. Though the story of Joseph revealed how and what God could do in the midst of dysfunction, God had an amazing plan for his life! Joseph's walk with God outweighed his family circumstances because he surrendered himself to God and chose a different path to be free of the confusion. Are you ready to choose a different path in your life? Surrender yourself to God because He will never leave you or forsake you (Deuteronomy 31:6). With God you are strong and courageous, so walk the path God has for you to leave dysfunction. God will lead you to become trustworthy, obedient to authority, safe, sexually pure and have a forgiving heart for all the hurt you have endured. In Genesis 50:20, Joseph stated to his brothers, "you intended to harm me, but God intended it for good". Right now, I can shout all by myself when I know how people have tried to hurt me by rejecting who I was as a Christian. Praise God for the good He has planned for our lives in the midst of the dysfunction around us. It is time for you to have a functional family!

HEALTHY IS AS HEALTHY DOES

A functional family is described on the website of hope-forheart.org as the following: "1) proper and mature behavior of 2 parents cultivates a healthy balance between individuality and relational skills among family members; 2) healthy emotional, psychological and spiritual growth cultivated among all family members; 3) family members encounter problems with the ability to face difficulties with confidence and support other family members". In a functional family, there is no denial or co-dependency which is usually demonstrated in a dysfunctional family. The dynamics of a dysfunctional family lead to unfulfilling relationships as adults.

The spiritually healthy functional family has an intimate relationship with Jesus Christ. This family seeks to understand and live a surrendered life to God's plan similar to Joseph. Through God's word, intimate prayers and being obedient listeners to Him, this family learn His plan for them, are convicted by the Holy Spirit to understand the different sin areas and allow forgiveness and grace to heal the broken places in their lives. They understand that without God's help and power they will not be able to live in peace or victory. Remember, there are benefits to a functional spiritual family which are: "flexibility, mutual love and respect; spiritual cooperation and offering love to one another".

It is time for you to have peace and victory over the dysfunction in your life with Jesus Christ in the center of everything. Allow Him to lead you out of the trenches of dysfunction and lean on Jesus all the time. He doesn't care how much you lean on Him as long as you are obedient to Him and His word. "You don't have to be a victim of your upbringing; a dysfunctional family can crush your self-esteem, confuse you and wreck your present and future relationships". Stop living on the edge because you are from a dysfunctional or difficult family! Break the cycle by destroying the root with Jesus Christ! Tell yourself, "dysfunction will stop with me" and mean what you are saying. Believe it most of all. Say, "I want to have a functional family unit as my legacy". There is hope for you today as you hand over the dysfunction to Jesus Christ and walk away. There will be some lonely days at the beginning and even on occasions, but peace of mind is the best victory you can have.

CHAPTER 7

MOUNTAINS OF BETRAYAL

"To me, the thing that is worse than death is betrayal. You see, I could conceive death, but I could not conceive betrayal." - Malcolm X

[Family] blood waters run deep...

"Blood is [definitely] thicker than water". Don't get it twisted! Although the majority of readers will undoubtedly believe this maxim to support the notion that (biological) family blood is thicker than water, I'm referring to the blood of Christ Jesus Who shed His blood for all humanity! It's indeed a blessing to know that you are blood related to the Savior Jesus Christ! However, the betrayal of a biological family member causes division and prolonged dysfunction than most would like to admit. Oddly enough, this occurs more often than we'd like to acknowledge.

Spousal betrayal stings to the core! Husbands and wives who commit adultery, whether emotional or physical, cause so much collateral damage and it's almost always irreparable without Christ. Selfishness, bitterness, pride and every evil work manifests while Satan's agenda promulgates like wildfire in a forest. The myriad of emotions one suffers after this type of abuse may contribute to prolonged feelings of anger, anxiety, fear, and low self-value. I'm only referring to professed believers in Christ at this point. The poison that contaminates the wounded spouse's perception of others both infects and affects other, otherwise healthy, relationships. Moreover, many accept a cynical perspective toward others' marriages and God's design for marriage.

As a wife, it's offensive when those closest to you habitually seek out adulterous relationships. And, although I've never experienced this type of betrayal; I take offense to those who disregard the sacred covenant between a husband and his wife! Listen, allow me to offer a disclaimer. I'm not referencing individuals who exhibited poor judgment once or twice but rather those who ignore the God's to seek out unavailable individuals. It has been my experience that these individuals are severely damaged. They typically do not possess a healthy spiritual relationship with God.

My family members have actively encouraged one another (and others) in multiple adulterous relationships. What's more is that they did so expecting me to both acknowledge and hide the betrayal. I must say that the betrayals revealed my masked emotions. Inwardly, I began to dislike not only the chosen behaviors but also the individual! How could I not support my family? I mean, we share the same "blood"! It wasn't difficult for me to comprehend how I, a former fornicator, liar, thief, and many other things, could become so easily offended. It was because unlike my (biological) family, I had truly begun to acknowledge Christ as my personal Savior and, I further realized that an accountability factor was required! Mine.

I had not held myself accountable to my [personal] convictions! I'd allowed myself to be bullied into supporting actions that I categorically abhorred. This began to form an increasing resentment toward me by my family members. I sensed "it". I resented "it"! I eventually loathed "it" and began to just ignore "it". "It" became a part of the "norm" and, even my children were exposed to "it". This incensed me because I'm a Christian, a married Christian.

I soon began to gradually distance myself and the tension increased. Soon enough, my allegiance to family was judged, questioned, and ridiculed. I was okay with that; after all, I'm an only child and was accustomed to living as "loner". You may not be familiar with this type of dysfunctional betrayal; however, you've undoubtedly witnessed its pervasive effects in and on [Christian] marriages.

The betrayals that ensued left me bewildered, wounded and yes, angry! At one point, the anger had begun to fuel bitterness! I didn't want to intercede for someone who could neither respect nor value my views. The egregious betrayal blindsided me but it also propelled me further info purpose! I thank God for Romans 8:28. Question, has someone you loved betrayed you or someone you love in this area? How did you respond then? Now?

I'm not attempting to sound crass or mean spirited. I only want to expose some of the dysfunctional behaviors that often manifest after a family betrayal. It would behoove anyone experiencing this form of betrayal to actually trust God's word concerning family betrayal. Wives and husbands alike contribute to dysfunctional family mountains of betrayal when either succumbs to the principality of adultery. Adultery is certainly not the only form of marital betrayal. However, adultery is a paramount factor in husband/wife betrayals. Sometimes, other family betrayals lie just under the surface.

For instance, another all too familiar mountain, mothers betraying daughters or daughters betraying mothers may arise and dissension [within the family dynamics] soon manifests. Invariably, this mountain continues to inundate the lives of so many women. I've not only experienced and conquered this mountain but I've also accepted the fact that the option to forgive was not truly an "option" but rather a mandate! Family betrayal is more common today as opposed to previous years. The degree of disrespect among children toward adults, especially [their] parents, is both alarming and disheartening.

Family betrayal reveals a level of dysfunction that may require years of counseling and self-evaluation. Even more specific is the mountain of betrayal demonstrated by a mother against her daughter. The statistics of dysfunctional mother/daughter relationships and interactions are staggering. Nonetheless, the awkward, rebellious "teen" years are one thing and, many mothers anticipate these "growing pains". Consequently, mothers [of daughters] across the board relate to this very sensitive topic.

Mothers who have lived lives of regret and unfulfillment tend to betray their daughters consistently and egregiously. These mothers may enjoy a fabricated or seemingly loving relationship with their daughters. However, many secretly covet the lives of their daughters. We cringe at the thought of any mother who would betray her daughter(s). Many of these mother's model behaviors they've witnessed in other women. Still others attempt to live vicariously through their daughters via control.

In dysfunctional families of betrayal, sibling betrayal yields yet another type of family deception. Sibling rivalry is one thing; betrayal is quite another. When a sibling betrays you, it may leave you befuddled and angry. Who hasn't witnessed or experienced sibling rivalry? It's an uneasy experience to witness, even from the outside looking in. Sibling betrayal manifests in numerous ways, from identity theft to adultery with the sibling's spouse. Okay, breathe. I realize that this a difficult pill to swallow. However, the fact remains that adultery does occur and, sometimes it's with the [betrayed] spouse's sibling.

These family betrayal mountains are most often rooted in sin. The rivalry oftentimes began generations ago. The twenty-fifth chapter of the book of Genesis records Adam and Eve's love experience. This union produced twins, Cain and Abel. The rivalry is evident in childhood and, eventually culminates in Abel's death at the hand of his [twin] brother Cain. How disturbing that siblings would end up so confused that the betrayal is that of death! Have you experienced sibling betrayal, either as the antagonist or the protagonist?

Cain and Abel weren't the only siblings who engaged in sibling rivalry and betrayal. Esau and Jacob experienced sibling rivalry and one, Jacob, manipulated the other, Esau. The betrayal was so practical yet diabolical! Like many of us, Jacob never saw it coming. Jacob was vulnerable. His vulnerability caused him to make a poor decision, a hasty decision, a life changing decision! This betrayal further fragmented the family dysfunction. Sibling rivalry continues today, even in the most productive Christian family.

Let's take a quick look at Leah and Rachel. Oh yes! Sibling rivalry among God's daughters occurs much to the chagrin of the parents. Genesis 29 shares the account of sisters Leah and Rachel. These sisters undoubtedly loved their parents and one another. However, Leah must have experienced enormous anxiety and pressure concerning marriage as she was the eldest of the two daughters. We are familiar with the biblical account. Laban consequently arranged for Jacob to wed his beloved youngest daughter, Rachel. However, Jacob married Leah instead. This betrayal angered Jacob and increased tensions in the family. Maybe you've never experienced this exact betrayal; however, the emotional distress that sibling betrayal causes is no less painful!

The movie Soul Food spins the sibling rivalry and betrayal experience. The two eldest sisters are at odds well into adulthood concerning actions that occurred when they were much younger. No great surprise that the two siblings' extended contention involves a man. Isn't that just like family! We hold grudges with one another but dare anyone [else] to begrudge our family. A word to the wise is sufficient! Betrayal, especially family betrayal, wreaks of darkness and involves the works of Satan.

Throughout the history of the Bible, we view the dysfunctional dynamics of betrayal through various lenses. Betrayal cuts like a knife, especially when you're on the receiving end of the betrayal! Betrayal befriends no one and backstabs everyone! No one is exempt from its grips; no one! Ponder this, betrayal betrays and loyalty commits.

Friends: The Bible indicates that "a friend sticketh closer than any brother". Sisters are a different story as in the aforementioned paragraphs! Although Jesus never directly refers to Judas as His friend, He does make reference to those in His inner circle. Jesus implies that we are indeed His friends. Judas's eventual betrayal of Jesus [for money] reveals just how commonplace betrayal is.

The old adage "Blood couldn't make us any closer" reveals the depth of the closeness between friends! Oh, but the pain of a friend's betrayal most certainly meets or exceeds that of a blood relative! When we allow ourselves to trust individuals outside of the family ties, we've undoubtedly done so in rich expectation of reciprocity! We're hopeful that the relationship is one of greater reward. Whether professional or personal, friends are those whom we've elected to invite into our lives.

When betrayal enters the relationship, it doesn't lessen the pain because they are not "blood related." The pain is both real and relevant. It's real in the sense that we can "feel" it. The emotional damage imposes feelings of despair, regret, anger, fear, mistrust and distrust. As believers growing into the knowledge of Christ Jesus, we should also encompass the feeling of love. After the initial shock wears off, prayer and love must be integrated into the equation. It is with love and kindness that Jesus won us to Himself, thereby reconciling us to the Heavenly Father! This is amazing! I'm excited to acknowledge this particular point. We must allow God to remake us. Remaking requires both love and forgiveness to move on.

Moving On

Are you prepared to move on? Often times, we say that we are prepared to move on. Nevertheless, our actions speak otherwise. Moving on requires intentional thoughts to do so coupled with deliberate actions that substantiate and facilitate the renewed mindset to move on. Moving on requires forgiveness because without it; there is no moving forward. Those who cannot forgive or refuse to forgive, invariably remain stuck. They're trapped in time until they decide to add forgiveness to the equation. Question, is forgiveness factored into your "moving on" equation?

As we move progressively forward, we must seek to improve our relationships while increasing our knowledge and love for humanity. Moving on requires personal accountability and responsibility. Moving on and up challenges us to be accountable not only to those in our circles but also ourselves. We must ask the question, "Why is [this] betrayal present in my life". Judas' betrayal of Jesus was ordained and served a specific purpose. Here's a thought, if you've experienced betrayal by a friend; what do you believe was the overall intended purpose? Although God does not cause these things to happen, He allowed it to transpire for some reason. Remember, Romans 8:28 holds the betrayed accountable for recognizing that both positive and negative experiences work together for our [ultimate] good!

Moving on also requires us to self-evaluate. Are you friendly? Do you present and represent yourself as one who can be a friend? Bishop T. D. Jakes is quoted as saying, "it takes commitment to be my friend". Oh wow, commitment is a powerful word. It's a word that either frightens individuals away or excites them to commitment. Are you able to commit to friendship? Why? Why not?

Moving on is painful, challenging and life changing! It's time. Let's do it...together.

CHAPTER 8

MOUNTAINS OF UNFORGIVENESS
CONTRIBUTED BY: GABRIELLE CRUMP

"Forgiveness is me giving up my right to hurt you for hurting me."- Anonymous

To Forgive or Not to Forgive...

"Forgiveness does not change the past, but it does change the future." Forgiveness is a tough subject for many people. Whether you've been the victim of a hurtful situation or you've hurt someone, forgiveness is a topic that can strike a nerve at any given moment. The bible mentions forgiveness (in different variations; forgive, forgiven, etc.) over 100 times. Forgiveness is the foundation in which salvation is built. So why do so many live their lives as if forgiveness is an option? As if forgiveness is a burden and not a blessing? Forgiveness is an act of love, one that cost nothing more than openness of heart and mind. So how does someone who's been hurt beyond their limit of forgiveness, learn to forgive? What happens before we forgive? Once we forgive? And after we forgive? Are the words "I'm sorry", really the magic words that unlock the door to the forgiving heart, or is there much more to it?

ACKNOWLEDGEMENT

The first step in moving any mountain in our lives always begins with acknowledgment. Acknowledging that there is a mountain of un-forgiveness that stands between you and living a purposeful life, is the very first step of this mountain moving process. Sometimes that acknowledging means facing a very painful past, an agonizing act, or reliving a very traumatic experience. This can be tough for anyone especially one who feels as if they have been hurt beyond the point of repair. "How do I forgive the man/woman who sexually abused me?" "How do I forgive my spouse for cheating on me and leaving me for someone else?" "How do I forgive my business partner for leaving me in debt I didn't create?" "How do I forgive the person who killed my loved one?" are all questions that fill the hearts of many who have been the victim of hurt and pain. And the hard truth is, you do it by realizing you have been forgiven and because of God's loving kindness should also forgive those that have hurt you. Don't misunderstand me however, God's forgiveness of our sins is not contingent upon our forgiving others, but He forgives us and extends a great degree of grace that we may see the beauty in forgiveness.

However, acknowledgment goes beyond stating the truth about the mountain that stands before you. Acknowledgement is also realizing that forgiveness goes far beyond hearing the words "I'm sorry" because sometimes you never will. Consider the person who was physically abused by a parent for years. They live a life full of anger and resentment towards that parent because the parent never apologized for those years of abuse. One day they receive a phone call that the parent has died. Do they continue to walk with an attitude of anger and a heart that refuses to forgive? The parent never said sorry and now, will never be able to because they no longer have the chance to. There are so many situations in which waiting to hear a person apologize for what they've done to you is frankly not an option. But should that keep you at the base of your mountain, unable to move it because you are unable to forgive? We have all heard the cliché "Forgiveness isn't for the other person it's for you". This is truer than you can ever imagine. What if the only thing standing between you and peace, you and joy, you and purpose, is a mere condition of the heart?

IT'S A CHOICE

"Everyone says forgiveness is a lovely idea, until they have something to forgive." - C.S. Lewis

This quote rings true to anyone who stands before a towering mountain of un-forgiveness. When you make a conscious decision to forgive someone who has caused you tremendous pain, you take the second step towards moving the mountain of un-forgiveness. What many people fail to realize is the self-destruction that results from an un-forgiving heart. I've heard stories and testimonies time and time again of people who spent years being unwilling to forgive and because of this choice they made, they spent many years in a state of depression, denial, and their health was even compromised.

When you choose not to forgive, you choose to continue to let your mountain of un-forgiveness grow. And just like the avalanche that can occur at any time, taking with it anything in its path, un-forgiveness does the same in our lives. It destroys our trust and our faith in God. It ruins families. It causes health problems that otherwise wouldn't be if we simply made the right choice. Contrary to popular belief, when a person chooses to hurt you they aren't the one that holds the power, you are. In fact, you have the upper hand in the situation. You can either choose to hold on to the pain, the fear, the nightmare of the occurrence and waste years in misery, or you can choose to forgive and experience the beauty in having a peace of mind, a light heart, and a life with purpose! "What purpose?" you ask, purpose in sharing the freedom in forgiving. Satan knows that as long as he can keep your mind focused on what happened to you, you'll never focus on what God can use it to do **THROUGH** you. (Go back and read that one more time). When you are free to forgive, you are free to share the story of how you not only approached a mountain you deemed impossible to move, but in fact moved it! And it was all because you made a choice to not hold on to the story but to free your heart to share it.

A painful past and forgiveness are a lot like a sore or scab on your arm. The longer you keep it bandaged only opening it to see the wound the longer it takes it to heal. But the moment you remove the bandage and apply the ointment and allow it to begin to heal the sooner it heals and the sooner your skin recovers back to the way it once looked. A lot of people will say "that's easier said than done", but it really isn't. Forgiveness is as easy as saying in your heart... "I choose to forgive you for what you did. Not solely for you, but for me, for my destiny, my purpose, and my future." Really, it is just that simple. Try it. Take a minute to really condition your heart to picture your life free of the guilt, pain, and agony of being chained to the mountain of un-forgiveness, and just say it! Make the choice and speak forgiveness over your life and over your past and watch the walls begin to fall.

THE AFTERMATH

We can all agree that forgiveness can be a beautiful and life changing experience. But what happens once you've forgiven a person? What does life look like during the aftermath of forgiveness? Do things just magically go back to normal? Do you reconnect with the person or people who hurt you as if nothing ever happened? And once you have finally forgiven, is the mountain moving process complete?

By no means is forgiveness ever a "swept under the rug" phenomena. Once forgiveness has taken place in your heart, things may still look and feel the same for a while. The pain may still linger for a little while, because let's just be frank, we aren't God. We can't throw another person's wrongdoings into the sea of forgetfulness and remember them no more. The harsh reality is that those memories may forever be a part of who we are. They inadvertently make us who we are. So how does life change after your heart has forgiven? What does it feel like? How do you know it's been done... for real? When you have forgiven a person for something they did that caused you to spend nights crying and years distraught the one sure way you know you've forgiven them is by how you respond to them. If a person says their name around you, you don't fill up inside with overpowering rage, you don't think of a million ways you could hurt them or get revenge. Instead there is a peace in the way you breathe, think, and respond to not only hearing that person's name, but being in their presence.

I can remember times before I had forgiven my biological father for abandoning me and all the hurtful things he'd done and said. When people would mention him I could feel the anger boiling hot in my heart. I would tense up and become extremely defensive and almost always would respond in an angry tone, asking why his name had to be mentioned. If I happened to run into him in a common place, my heart would begin to pound and my fists would clinch because I could not stand the sight of him. I would spend nights furiously thinking about ways I wished he could feel the pain I'd felt from the choices he'd made concerning me. I spent so many years battling migraine headaches, and I feel that it was due in part to my un-forgiving heart. But oh when God reconditioned my heart and allowed me to experience the peace that steamed from forgiveness. I could talk freely about him. I could bring his name up and not feel angry or irritated at the thought. If I ran into him I was able to speak and carry on with my life and he no longer controlled the winds in my life. You see when you've truly forgiven a person you can accept what they did and who they are even if you never hear the words "I'm sorry" part from their lips. I had spent so long focused on waiting to hear something I probably never would; I didn't even realize just how fast life was passing me by.

When you forgive someone, it doesn't mean you have to return to in common fellowship with them. Again, keep in mind that forgiveness is primarily for you and no one else. Don't allow others to dictate how you should go about forgiving a person. People will tell you that forgiveness means being back on speaking terms with the person who hurt you and that's just not true. You must use discernment to help you decide whether or not reconnecting with someone who's hurt you, is the best thing for you. If a person has not changed and you can sense there's even the slightest potential for them to strike again, it may not be in your best interest to align yourself with them. People who have not made up in their own hearts and minds to change will continue to hurt you if given the opportunity. The abusive husband, who has not sought professional help, may still have tendencies to abuse his estranged wife. The gossiping mother, who has not reconditioned her heart, may still pose a problem for the broken child who was affected by slanderous words. The lying father, who still has yet to keep a promise, may compromise the relationship if given another opportunity to start again. At the end of the day, it is up to you, through discernment to decide if a person is ready to have a renewed relationship with you. If you decided it's best to forgive and deal with a person from a distance, do that and don't feel bad about it. The thing about the mountain of un-forgiveness is that even after you have forgiven a person, Satan will still attempt to distract you with other worries, such as, "do I need to be back in regular fellowship with this person". If you spend time wondering whether or not to call the person who hurt you on a daily basis, or if you should let them back into the inner circle of your life, you're not focusing on purpose, you're still focused on that person.

THE FINAL ACT OF LOVE

"Forgiveness is the final act of love." Reinhold Niebuhr

Forgiveness is a beautiful gift you can not only receive but freely give. Forgiving someone who hurt you, forgiving yourself for poor decision making, are both freeing methods by which mountains can be moved from your life. A mountain of un-forgiveness can spring from another mountain they may be attempting to distract you from fulfilling your God given purpose. But the mountain of un-forgiveness can also create other mountains if not removed in a timely and proper manner. The freedom found in moving your mountain of un-forgiveness is making the final decision, that you no longer wish to hold on to the wound or wounds of the past. And in every essence it is truly the final act of love.

When we make a conscious decision to act in love and forgive, we are ultimately making a choice to follow in the steps of our Creator. God forgives us time and time again, without holding it over our heads, without removing the grace He extends; He does it, because He loves us. Making a decision to forgive is saying to God, "I trust you to heal me and help me and be Lord over my life including my past, my present, and my future." Forgiveness is saying I may not forget what you did or what I did (to myself), but I choose to move beyond it, thereby moving the mountain I thought would stand before me for the rest of my life. Imagine your life full of the joy and peace you desire. If you like what you see, take the steps towards moving your mountain of un-forgiveness and let God show you the beauty in true forgiveness.

[Dear Heavenly Father, I realize I have spent years lamenting over the pain from my past, but not only have I focused on the pain, I've focused on the source of that pain, which has caused my heart to become cold, and a mountain to form before me. God I ask that you in your loving kindness would first forgive me, for refusing to forgive the person who has hurt me. Now I ask that you would lead me in my own path of forgiving. Recondition my heart and open my spiritual eyes to see this situation how you would have me to see it. Remove the anger, the revengeful spirit, the negative attitudes, and the feelings of pain from my heart. Lord I trust you to help me through my healing process and through my own personal process of forgiveness. I forgive **(CALL THE PERSON(S) BY NAME) for (CALL OUT THE ACT IN WHICH YOU ARE FORGIVING)** and I ask that you would restore my view of them. I understand that forgiveness does not mean reconnecting but that forgiving them is a matter of my heart and I thank you that I no longer allow them or what they did to me, to deter me from fulfilling my purpose in you. Finally, Lord help me to use my story of forgiveness to share with others who may battle with the same mountain. Send me where I need to go to inspire someone else to forgive. Thank you for teaching me about forgiveness that I may forgive someone else. In Christ Jesus' name, Amen].

CHAPTER 9

THE MOUNTAIN MOVERS 31 DAY DEVOTIONAL AND INTERACTIVE PRAYER GUIDE

**Thirty-One Days of Mountain Moving Prayers
(that will reshape and transform your thinking)**

The comprehensive objective of this devotional is to challenge the reader to actively change her attitude and mindset concerning dysfunction through the word of God. Additionally, this 31 day devotional sets a mental tone conducive to spiritual growth and awakening through: accountability, responsibility, acknowledgement, and effective communication.

Day 1: Psalm 91

He that dwelleth in the secret place of the most High shall abide under the shadow of the Almighty. – Psalm 91

What mountain caused this scripture to become relative in my life?

_____

_____

_____

_____

_____

_____

_____

_____

_____

_____

_____

_____

_____

_____

_____

_____

_____

_____

_____

_____

_____

_____

_____

_____

_____

Day 2: Psalm 23

The Lord is my shepherd; I shall not want. – Psalm 23

What mountain caused me to recognize the Lord as my Shepherd?

_____

_____

_____

_____

_____

_____

_____

_____

_____

_____

_____

How did this experience change me?

_____

_____

_____

_____

_____

_____

_____

_____

_____

_____

_____

_____

_____

Day 3: Psalm 34

I will bless the Lord at all times: his praise shall continually be in my mouth. – *Psalm 34*

How difficult was it for me to bless the Lord during challenging times?

_____

_____

_____

_____

_____

_____

_____

_____

_____

_____

_____

_____

_____

_____

_____

_____

_____

_____

_____

_____

_____

_____

_____

_____

Day 4: Matthew 6:12-15

And forgive us our debts, as we forgive our debtors.

And lead us not into temptation, but deliver us from evil: For thine is the kingdom, and the power, and the glory, forever. Amen. For if ye forgive men their trespasses, your heavenly Father will also forgive you: But if ye forgive not men their trespasses, neither will your Father forgive your trespasses. Matthew 6:12-15

Have I forgiven those who created mountains in my life?

_____

_____

_____

_____

_____

_____

_____

_____

_____

_____

_____

_____

_____

_____

_____

_____

_____

_____

_____

_____

_____

Day 5: Matthew 21:21

Jesus answered and said unto them, Verily I say unto you, If ye have faith, and doubt not, ye shall not only do this which is done to the fig tree, but also if ye shall say unto this mountain, Be thou removed, and be thou cast into the. – Matthew 21:21

Am I continuing to fear the greatness of the mountain or do I believe I can conquer it? Is this scripture applicable?

_____

_____

_____

_____

_____

_____

_____

_____

_____

_____

_____

_____

_____

_____

_____

_____

_____

_____

_____

_____

Day 6: I Peter 5:7

Casting all your care upon him; for he careth for you. – 1 Peter 5:7

Have I casted my fear of specific mountains upon Jesus?

_____
_____
_____
_____
_____
_____
_____
_____
_____
_____
_____
_____
_____
_____
_____
_____
_____
_____
_____
_____
_____
_____
_____
_____
_____

Day 7: Isaiah 53:4-5

Surely he hath borne our griefs, and carried our sorrows: yet we did esteem him stricken, smitten of God, and afflicted. But he was wounded for our transgressions, he was bruised for our iniquities: the chastisement of our peace was upon him; and with his stripes we are healed
– Isaiah 53:4-5

Do I truly possess peace about the mountains in my life? Why? Why not?

_____

_____

_____

_____

_____

_____

_____

_____

_____

_____

_____

_____

_____

_____

_____

_____

_____

_____

_____

_____

_____

_____

Day 8: Isaiah 55:9-11

For as the heavens are higher than the earth, so are my ways higher than your ways, and my thoughts than your thoughts. For as the rain cometh down, and the snow from heaven, and returneth not thither, but watereth the earth, and maketh it bring forth and bud, that it may give seed to the sower, and bread to the eater: So shall my word be that goeth forth out of my mouth: it shall not return unto me void, but it shall accomplish that which I please, and it shall prosper in the thing whereto I sent it. – Isaiah 55:9-11

Are the mountains prospering in my life or is God's word prospering? Why?

_____

_____

_____

_____

_____

_____

_____

_____

_____

_____

_____

_____

_____

_____

_____

_____

_____

_____

Day 9: Exodus 20:5

Thou shalt not bow down thyself to them, nor serve them: for I the Lord thy God am a jealous God, visiting the iniquity of the fathers upon the children unto the third and fourth generation of them that hate me;
- Exodus20:5

List the "generational" mountains you recognize in your family. What have you done to eradicate their formation in future generations?

_____

_____

_____

_____

_____

_____

_____

_____

_____

_____

_____

_____

_____

_____

_____

_____

_____

_____

_____

_____

_____

Day 10: James 1:22

But be ye doers of the word, and not hearers only, deceiving your own selves. – Janes 1:22

Am I actively applying God's word to my life concerning mountain moving?

_____
_____
_____
_____
_____
_____
_____
_____
_____
_____
_____
_____
_____
_____
_____
_____
_____
_____
_____
_____
_____
_____
_____
_____

Day 11: Luke 6:27-28

But I say unto you which hear, love your enemies, do good to them which hate you, Bless them that curse you, and pray for them which despitefully use you. – Luke 6:27-28

Do mountains of unforgiveness remain in my life? If so, what is the source of the pain concerning that mountain?

_____

_____

_____

_____

_____

_____

_____

_____

_____

_____

_____

_____

_____

_____

_____

_____

_____

_____

_____

_____

_____

_____

Day 12: Romans 12:1-2

I beseech you therefore, brethren, by the mercies of God, that ye present your bodies a living sacrifice, holy, acceptable unto God, which is your reasonable service. And be not conformed to this world: but be ye transformed by the renewing of your mind, that ye may prove what is that good, and acceptable, and perfect, will of God. – Romans 12:1-2

List any identifiable mountains that prevent you from presenting your body as "living sacrifices" to God.

_____

_____

_____

_____

_____

_____

_____

_____

_____

_____

_____

_____

_____

_____

_____

_____

_____

_____

_____

_____

_____

Day 13: Psalm 41:9

Yea, mine own familiar friend, in whom I trusted, which did eat of my bread, hath lifted up his heel against me. – Psalm 41:9

How has the mountain of betrayal altered my trust in God or people?

_____
_____
_____
_____
_____
_____
_____
_____
_____
_____
_____
_____
_____
_____
_____
_____
_____
_____
_____
_____
_____
_____
_____

Day 14: Matthew 10:21

And the brother shall deliver up the brother to death, and the father the child: and the children shall rise up against their parents, and cause them. – Matthew 10:21

Is this mountain hindering me...today? Why? Why not?

_____

_____

_____

_____

_____

_____

_____

_____

_____

_____

_____

_____

_____

_____

_____

_____

_____

_____

_____

_____

_____

_____

Day 15: Jeremiah 12:6

For even thy brethren, and the house of thy father, even they have dealt treacherously with thee; yea, they have called a multitude after thee: believe them not, though they speak fair words unto thee.
– Jeremiah 12:16

What types of family betrayal caused mountains to form in my life?

_____

_____

_____

_____

_____

_____

_____

_____

_____

_____

_____

_____

_____

_____

_____

_____

_____

_____

_____

_____

_____

Day 16: Matthew 26:24

The Son of man goeth as it is written of him: but woe unto that man by whom the Son of man is betrayed! it had been good for that man if he had not been born. – Matthew 26:24

Have I betrayed a friend for which I require forgiveness? Has this betrayal caused a mountain in my life?

_____

_____

_____

_____

_____

_____

_____

_____

_____

_____

_____

_____

_____

_____

_____

_____

_____

_____

_____

_____

_____

_____

_____

Day 17: Proverbs 10:12

Hatred stirs up strife, but love covers all wrongs. – Proverbs 10:12

Has the mountain of "hatred" eclipsed my other emotions, thereby hindering my love walk as a born again believer?

_____

_____

_____

_____

_____

_____

_____

_____

_____

_____

_____

_____

_____

_____

_____

_____

_____

_____

_____

_____

_____

_____

_____

_____

_____

Day 18: Proverbs 29:22

An angry man stirs up strife, and a wrathful man abounds in sin
– Proverbs 29:22

What is the root of the emotional mountains in my life? List your next "action" steps to conquer this mountain.

_____

_____

_____

_____

_____

_____

_____

_____

_____

_____

_____

_____

_____

_____

_____

_____

_____

_____

_____

_____

_____

_____

_____

_____

_____

_____

Day 19: Mark 3:25

If a house is divided against itself, that house cannot stand. –
Mark 3:25

What family dysfunctions can be traced back to other family generations? Have I spoken (confronted) these mountains? What was the outcome?

_____
_____
_____
_____
_____
_____
_____
_____
_____
_____
_____
_____
_____
_____
_____
_____
_____
_____
_____
_____
_____
_____
_____
_____

Day 20: Ecclesiastes 5:10

Whoever loves money never has enough; whoever loves wealth is never satisfied with their income. This too is meaningless. – Ecclesiastes 5:10

List any financial mountains that caused fear and distress. Have you overcome this mountain? Why? Why not?

_____

_____

_____

_____

_____

_____

_____

_____

_____

_____

_____

_____

_____

_____

_____

_____

_____

_____

_____

_____

_____

_____

_____

Day 21: Romans 13:18

Let no debt remain outstanding, except the continuing debt to love one another, for whoever loves others has fulfilled the law.
— Romans 13:18

How has poor financial stewardship stagnated my prosperity? How did this molehill develop info such a massive mountain?

_____

_____

_____

_____

_____

_____

_____

_____

_____

_____

_____

_____

_____

_____

_____

_____

_____

_____

_____

_____

_____

_____

Day 22: Habakkuk 2:2

The LORD answered me and said, write the vision, and make it a plan upon tables, that he may run that readeth it. – Habakkuk 2:2.

What vision has God given you? What are you actively doing with the vision to bless others and glorify God while abandoning former dysfunctional patterns?

_____

_____

_____

_____

_____

_____

_____

_____

_____

_____

_____

_____

_____

_____

_____

_____

_____

_____

_____

_____

_____

_____

Day 23: 1 John 1:9

If we confess our sins, he is faithful and just and will forgive us our sins and purify us from all unrighteousness. – 1 John 1:19

What sins continue to haunt you? Why? Does this sin prevent you from acknowledging mountains that arise?

_____

_____

_____

_____

_____

_____

_____

_____

_____

_____

_____

_____

_____

_____

_____

_____

_____

_____

_____

_____

_____

_____

_____

Day 24: Exodus 20:5

Thou shalt not bow down thyself to them, nor serve them: for I the Lord thy God am a jealous God, visiting the iniquity of the fathers upon the children unto the third and fourth generation of them that hate me. — *Exodus 20:5*

Do you believe you're facing a familiar mountain and are fearful to authoritatively speak to it? What is the (generational) mountain that impedes your purpose?

_____

_____

_____

_____

_____

_____

_____

_____

_____

_____

_____

_____

_____

_____

_____

_____

_____

_____

_____

_____

_____

Day 25: John 3:16

For God so loved the world, that he gave his only begotten Son, that whosoever believeth in him should not perish, but have everlasting life. - John 3:16

Do you believe that Christ died for your sins and that you are able to move forward without the guilt and/or embarrassment mountain of your past?

_____
_____
_____
_____
_____
_____
_____
_____
_____
_____
_____
_____
_____
_____
_____
_____
_____
_____
_____
_____

Day 26: 1 Corinthians 10:13

There hath no temptation taken you but such as is common to man: but God is faithful, who will not suffer you to be tempted above that ye are able; but will with the temptation also make a way to escape, that ye may be able to bear it. – 1 Corinthians 10:13

Is the peace of God ruling on your heart or has the mountain of fear and self-worth overtaken you?

_____
_____
_____
_____
_____
_____
_____
_____
_____
_____
_____
_____
_____
_____
_____
_____
_____
_____
_____
_____
_____
_____

Day 27: Matthew 17:20

"You don't have enough faith," Jesus told them. "I tell you the truth, if you had faith, even as small as a mustard seed, you could day to this mountain, 'move from here to here,' and it would move. Nothing would be impossible. – Matthew 17:20

What mountains have you identified and conquered in your life?

_____

_____

_____

_____

_____

_____

_____

_____

_____

_____

_____

_____

_____

_____

_____

_____

_____

_____

_____

_____

_____

_____

_____

Day 28: Psalm 46:1

God is our refuge and strength, a great help in times of distress. Psalm 46:1.

What mountain has Jehovah blessed you to avoid that (other) family members have endured/experienced?

_____

_____

_____

_____

_____

_____

_____

_____

_____

_____

_____

_____

_____

_____

_____

_____

_____

_____

_____

_____

_____

_____

_____

_____

Day 29: Romans 8:17

And since we are his children, we are his heirs. In fact, together with Christ we are heirs of God's glory. But if we are to share his glory, we must also suffer. – Romans 8:17

Do you believe that some mountains may be a part of your suffering? Do you believe that you are victorious in the suffering? Why or why not?

_____

_____

_____

_____

_____

_____

_____

_____

_____

_____

_____

_____

_____

_____

_____

_____

_____

_____

_____

_____

_____

Day 30: Galatians 5:7

Ye did run well; who did hinder you that ye should not obey the truth? - Galatians 5:7

Is there a particular mountain that you continue to climb?

_____

_____

_____

_____

_____

_____

_____

_____

_____

_____

_____

_____

_____

_____

_____

_____

_____

_____

_____

_____

_____

_____

_____

_____

_____

Day 31: Isaiah 53:1

Who hath believed our report? And to whom is the arm of the LORD? - Isaiah 53:1

Do you believe God's report concerning your mountains or the world's?

_____

_____

_____

_____

_____

_____

_____

_____

_____

_____

_____

_____

_____

_____

_____

_____

_____

_____

_____

_____

_____

_____

_____

ABOUT THE AUTHOR

Dr. C. Denise Richardson, women's and children's abuse prevention proponent, humanitarian, community leader, freelance writer, author, Life Strategist, ordained minister, former public school educator, administrator and Ex. Director of CDR Unlimited, is a survivor of both child sexual abuse (CSA)

and domestic violence (DV). C. Denise inspires women to confront personal and professional mountains in order to transform into women of prayer, power, purpose and prosperity! These four pillars correlate to individual and corporate legacies! C. Denise inspires women to activate/awaken purpose for themselves and others! #MountainMovers and #PurposeShakers are her most notable conferences. Dr. C. also offers monthly MastHERmind sessions for the aforementioned conference titles. Dr. C. loves women and is a radical catalyst for life, love, & legacy through accountability, faith, application, & collaboration!

Dr. Richardson is the self-proclaimed "Mountain Mover" and quintessential women's "Purpose Shakers" aficionado! Dr. C. enjoys bridging the gap among women of all cultures, educational backgrounds, professions, religions, and ethnicities. Invariably, she organizes both business symposiums and spiritual conferences to promote sisterhood and empowerment among women. Her two most affluential events are "Mountain Movers" and "Purpose Shakers".

C. Denise earned four degrees that include one undergrad, two masters, & one doctoral degree. Additionally, C. Denise has acquired numerous #CEUs in education, psychology, and counseling. Her commendations include community activism and philanthropy. C. Denise is also a member of various, notable community organizations.

www.cdrunlimited.com
C Denise Richardson: Facebook
DrCDenise: Twitter, Instagram & Periscope
CDRunlimited: Pinterest

Made in the USA
Charleston, SC
19 October 2016